W9-CQD-394

Acknowledgments

To my wife, Theresa and our three amazing children, Eli, Grace & Sophia. Thank you for your encouragement and love. I am so thankful that God brought us together as a family. It's a joy and honor to share life with you.

God, thank you for placing in me the desire to help others so I can help equip students for career and life success while following the example set by your son, Christ. Help Others In All That We Do!
Mark 10:45

A portion of the proceeds from every book sold will go to charity.

Contents

Background

I remember my senior year of college vividly, it has not been that long ago. I was enjoying the college life which included late classes so I could sleep in and no classes on Fridays, if at all possible. In my senior year I met the woman I wanted to spend the rest of my life with. Life was great but things were about to change. As I got closer to graduation I realized the sleeping in was almost over. The lazy afternoons mixed with studying and sometimes a little work was just about gone.

As I started the second semester of my senior year I began interviewing with multiple companies. I had a vision of walking into my first day of work with my briefcase by my side, new shoes and a new suit and tie that fit perfectly. In my mind I would be escorted to my new office on the corner of the 60th floor with a killer view. I could envision this so clearly as I prepared for my interviews. I was ready for life after college!

After interviewing for about a month I was offered a position and quickly accepted. I still had two months before graduating and had a job waiting. Life was good!

Just in case you are wondering if my vision of what my job would look like came true, let me just say, not exactly. My first job was with one of the largest poultry companies in the U.S. It was a chicken plant, not that there is anything wrong with that. My title was great, Plant Management Trainee. I was training to one day run a plant facility. I ended up trading in those new shoes for rubber boots, my suit and tie were replaced with jeans and a white lab coat. My brief case was a pocket in my lab coat filled with a pad, pen and anything else I may need. To round out the look I wore a hair net and a hard plastic bump hat. And my corner office was a metal locker.

I was up for the challenge and gave it everything I had. After a while though I realized I was not cut out for this type of work. I could not get the vision of a corporate job out of my head so soon after getting married to Theresa I left that position. I ended up moving back to Richmond I figured since I was from Richmond my chances of finding a job would be easy. Little did I know that the market had changed and jobs were very hard to come by. It was not quite as bad as today but it was pretty close. Because of this I had to come up with a way of separating myself from all the other people looking for work. I had to get away from the norm of just showing up with a resume. What I ended up creating was a personal Success Portfolio and I have been using it ever since. Because of my Success

Portfolio, whenever I would go for a promotion or interview for the same company or different one, I got the job. In fact it also allowed me to get larger raises as you will read about later.

For the majority of people, your first job won't be your last. You will be interviewing again sometime in the future. A person typically will have 10.5 jobs in their career, according to the U.S. Department of Labor's Bureau of Labor Statistics Report. Because of this, you need a document that will change as your experience changes. You are going to learn how to create your own personal Success Portfolio that will help keep you ahead of other people interviewing so you will be a top candidate and ultimately help you get the job.

All of this is what led me to creating a system that forever changed how I interviewed for a job. It allowed me to stand out from the crowd and get the job. It makes a lasting impression and will definitely make you stand out so people remember you. I remember one human resource manager pulling me to the side (this was after I had been with the company for 4 years and was up for my third promotion.) He brought me into his office and pulled down my Success Portfolio from his bookshelf that I used when interviewing with him for my first position four years earlier. He stated that it was the most impressive document anyone had brought to an interview.

I share this not to brag but to show you the importance of being able to separate yourself from the crowd so you stand out as the top candidate. It will leave a lasting impression that will make all the difference.

To close this section let me finish my story from earlier. It took a while before I got that corporate job and even then it was an entry level position. It did not take long however for me to climb the ladder of success. I used my Success Portfolio every step of the way and quickly moved up in the company. I had three promotions all within three years and was even having meetings with the vice president and president of the company.

Your success in your career and in life for that matter is within your reach. It will take work but with determination and desire you will be ready for success. So, if you are ready for the challenge and you're serious about taking control of your career, let's get started.

Introduction

"As long as you're going to think anyway, think big."
-Donald Trump

"God has given us two hands,
one to receive with and the other to give with."
- Billy Graham

Life is about to change so get ready! Since 2008 and up until the writing of this book there have been over 4.6 million jobs lost in the United States. Many college students are deciding to stay in school and get their graduate degree but at some point every student will begin interviewing and that's where this book will make all the difference. Through my years of experience interviewing people and through my research in talking with other individuals that interview and hire, it has become clear that there is one key issue that the majority of college students miss. This one thing makes all the difference in getting the job or not. Here it is, being able to effectively communicate your experience and skills in a way that sets you apart from everyone else. A resume is not enough anymore. You must take it to the next level to get noticed and GET HIRED!

I wrote this book for students who want to stand out from the crowd, get noticed and ultimately get hired. *Graduate With A Job* will help get it done. This book will help make the difference between an okay interview and one where you're a top candidate. It will make the difference between just taking the basic annual increase and getting the highest increase possible. Between being just another internal candidate for a promotion and being the top candidate.

One mistake most people make during an interview or review is not being able to promote their work and experience effectively. *Graduate With A Job* will not only share the importance of marketing yourself during a review or interview, it will give you step-by-step examples of how to accomplish this task. In the end, you will have created a this-is-your-life portfolio that will aid you in expressing your accomplishments. The importance of creating such a promotion portfolio is that it gives credibility to what you have done and backs it up with specific examples.

If you have ever been through an interview you know how stressful it can be. Trying to remember all the things you have covered in your preparation. Remembering all the examples to use when asked different questions can be overwhelming. By having your Success Portfolio with you, you take away almost all of that stress because the answers are in your portfolio. Think of it as your crib notes or an open book test. It's there to support your experience and skills and to use as a tool when answering questions so you don't have to keep everything locked in your mind.

This practical and easy-to-use book provides a clear and concise roadmap that will clearly set you apart from the crowd and help you get hired. This book will help you achieve your goals in ways only dreamed of. Furthermore, it guides you in setting up your own Success Portfolio. You will begin to separate your accomplishments into distinct categories, which will later make up your portfolio. The section on situational planning will go over questions you may be asked during an interview and will show how to answer them using your portfolio. You will be given scenarios such as getting a bigger raise; improving your chances for a promotion; getting the best review possible; interviewing like a pro, positioning your lack of experience; and how to effectively answer questions. In each scenario you will be given step-by-step instructions that will show you how to prepare, organize, and answer in a successful manner.

It is my hope that *Graduate With A Job* will provide you with the tools to better yourself and your situation. I wrote this book to allow you to read through it quickly and begin immediately implementing the ideas found here to create your own Success Portfolio. What I am sharing with you is something that, although simple, is rarely done or done correctly. I want to provide you with all the information you need without all the fluff you don't, so you can begin achieving your goals today.

As you begin, take time to think about your goals. What do you want to achieve? So many people don't take the time to just dream and really think about the goals they want to achieve. Take time to just dream. As minister, entrepreneur, and author Robert H. Schuller said, "What great thing would you attempt if you knew you could not fail?" What we see as failures or mistakes are actually taking us one step closer to success and reaching our goals. When we give up and stop taking chances for fear of failure, we stop growing.

Michael Jordan, basketball great, once said, "I have missed more than 9,000 shots in my career. I have lost almost 300 games. On twenty-six occasions I have been entrusted to take the game's winning shot...and missed. And I have failed over and over and over again in my life. And that is why...I succeed."

Look for ways to match your dreams and goals with helping others. How can you achieve your goals by helping others? If you keep others in mind as you're traveling down the road toward achieving your dreams, you will see amazing things happen. God did not create us to think only of our selves. We were created to help others. In fact, Christ was sent not to be served but to serve. The way to true happiness and success is found when we put others ahead of ourselves.

"For even the Son of Man came not to be served but to serve
others and to give his life as a ransom for many."
Mark 10:45 (NLT)

Have you ever noticed that when you take your focus off yourself and your situation and place it on others that are less fortunate how your perspective changes. When you find yourself feeling down, frustrated or just plain stressed, look for a way to help others. As you gain success in your career look for ways to take others along. If we live our lives for others we then find the true purpose and passion Christ has for us.

Take every opportunity to pursue your dreams. Don't settle for the limitations that others may set for you. Dream big and then take action to make your dreams a reality. It's time to start taking control of your success!

"From what we get, we can make a living;
what we give, however, makes a life."
-Arthur Ashe

1

The Most Important Chapter
For Career & Life Success

Throughout this book you will learn breakthrough strategies and techniques for standing out from the crowd when interviewing that will help you be a top candidate. You are getting ready to learn how to create a personal Success Portfolio that will forever change how you interview, go for promotions and even how you receive a raise. But if that is all I share with you in this book, I will consider it a failure.

The bottom line I want to get across to you is that God created you for a purpose & for success. He wants you to succeed and do great things.

"Delight in me and I will give you the desires of your heart."
–Psalm 37:4

You will soon enter the workforce and begin mapping the course for your career. There are many ways you can go about this and there is no one right answer but here is the thing, experience life. The life God has for you. That may mean working for a company or it may mean starting your own company. It could mean being a stay at home mom once you decide to have children. It could mean doing something totally different than what you ever considered or have even gone to school for. Be open to where God leads you. Be ready for the experience.

So what does this have to do with career and life success you may be asking, everything! As you begin your career look for where God is leading you and how you can help others along the way. Did you catch it? Help others along the way. That is the key to true success. When you are in it just for you, when you are looking out for number one you will in many cases achieve the goal you set out to achieve while missing the real target. Achieving the goal, making the money, buying the house, car and whatever else you want to buy provides some satisfaction but if that is all your living your life for you will soon feel empty. There will always be a new goal to achieve, more money to make, new things to buy. You make a new goal and do everything you can to achieve it only to realize it's not enough. As long as your goals are only about you, you won't find true purpose, success and satisfaction. On the other hand, when you start to look for ways to help others on your journey to achieving your goals everything changes.

"There is more happiness in giving than receiving."
-Acts, 20:35

"The more I help others to succeed, the more I succeed."
-Ray Kroc

"In helping others, we shall help ourselves, for whatever good we give out completes the circle and comes back to us."
-Flora Edwards

Don't get caught up in only the big things in life. It can be the simple acts of kindness that make a huge difference in someone else's life. Always look for ways to help others! Look for ways to help others in everything you do, especially when you are feeling down on yourself. Focus on others. When you feel like you have no place to go and no one to turn to, focus on others. When you are sad, focus on others. When you are having a pity party for yourself, focus on others. What do I mean when I say focus on others? I mean look for ways to help someone else. The moment you begin to look for ways to help others you begin to feel better. That's because you take the focus off of you and put it on someone else. If we all begin to look out for each other instead of just ourselves, think of all that can be achieved.

Remember, as you set your goals for success, set them looking at how you can do your job while helping others. Believe me; it *will* make all the difference in the world! No matter if you are an investment broker, realtor, sales professional, teacher, manager, mother, father, business owner, or anything else, if you set your goal to make money and becoming rich, you may be happy in the short term, but in the long run you will have a life without purpose and one that is never fulfilled. There is absolutely nothing wrong with making money—heck, this book is about improving yourself, your position, and your *pay*—but if that is the ultimate goal, then you will be sadly missing the bigger picture and the ultimate happiness and purpose for your life.

"If you help enough other people get what they want, you will always achieve what you want."
-Zig Ziglar

No matter what you do for your career, do it for others. If you build relationships first and put the focus on helping those around you, you will come to realize that what's truly important is not how much money you make, but how you have helped someone else. And in this you will receive more than you could ever imagine.

You are the future leaders of this great country. Lead by example and show the world that true leadership does not step on others and push them down as you strive to reach our goals. True leadership and success comes from helping others achieve and reach their goals while you are on your own journey to achieving your goals.

Believe in yourself and your abilities. Know that God created you and has great plans for you so dare to try new things, and enjoy the experience. I wish you all the success in your future endeavors.

God Bless.

Stephen

Check out *www.GraduateWithAJob.com* for great tips on interviewing. It's also a great place to ask questions and respond to information I share as you get ready to GET HIRED!

2

The Importance of Promoting Your Accomplishments

"People are always blaming their circumstances for what they are. I don't believe in circumstances. The people who get on in this world are the people who get up and look for the circumstances they want, and if they can't find them, they make them."
-George Bernard Shaw

In times of uncertainty with job cuts, reorganizations, downsizing, and smaller pay raises, many people feel they don't have control of their future. As you prepare to graduate and go out into the working world you may not feel you have the experience needed to get the type of job you really want. For this reason, it's imperative that you take the next step in improving your future and follow the steps outlined in this book.

Let's walk through a couple of scenarios that you will be ready for. Some of these will come later in your career. You arrive at your interview ready for whatever they throw your way. They start asking about experience and, well, how can they expect you to have real experience when you have been in school for four or more years? It's that old dilemma: you need experience, but how can you get experience if no one will hire you? In this book you will learn how to take your experience while in school and turn it into real world examples.

Here is another example. You have been with a company for a year and your meeting with your manager to go over your yearly review. Your manager begins to review some information the company has on your performance. She or he asks some questions on how you think things are going and then shares how things are *really* going. You chime in with items you worked on throughout the year and your manager agrees that those were very positive. You hope to be getting a good increase in pay, say an 8-10% increase, because you have done such a solid job for the company. That's when you get the news that things have been tight and they only have a certain percentage to share among all employees, so your annual increase will be 2.5% this year. Is there anything you can do now to up that percentage? Yes! You will learn how later in the book.

Let's go over one more scenario. You're interviewing for your first job or maybe a future promotion with the same company or a new one. You have read all the books on answering every question possible and have plenty of copies of your résumé on hand. You have wiped the sweat from your palms and are ready to go. As you sit down, it begins: the inquisition. You feel like a contestant on *Jeopardy,* question after question asked of you and you don't know if you have the right answer.

As the employer begins asking you question after question, you answer to the best of your ability. She asks for examples and you

provide some, but you're not sure if you have provided enough information. You're trying to remember all the examples you had prac-
ticed but they are just not coming to you. Maybe it's because of the
stress your feeling. After all is said and done, you leave the interview
wondering what the interviewer is thinking, how you could have
answered better, and how you forgot to mention those three examples
you worked so hard on preparing. You leave hoping for the best but
not quite sure how things will turn out, knowing that there are ten
other people vying for the same position. Is there something you
could have done differently to ensure you'd leave with confidence? Is
there something you could have done to wipe away the stress and
make sure you don't forget any example? Yes!

> *"I have always looked at an interview as an opportunity to
> sell the product people know best…themselves. It's critical
> that candidates come to an interview fully prepared to be able to docu-
> ment their successes and present this information with impact. A "Suc-
> cess Portfolio" will help the candidate back up what they are saying and
> will set them apart."*
> **-Michael Redding, Senior District Sales Manager,
> Major U.S. Pharmaceutical Company**

As I was preparing to graduate from college, my father told
me to pick the company I wanted to work for and simply start working. Soon after coming out of the military and serving in World War
II, he walked into a company, filled out an application, and forty-two

years later retired with full benefits. His concept on working for a company was that you work for the same one until you retire, but that's not exactly how things work these days. As I mentioned in the Background section, the average person born in the later years of the baby boom held 10.5 jobs from age eighteen to age forty. Nearly three-fifths of these jobs were held from ages eighteen to twenty-five. Security at a position until you retire is a thing of the past now that we live in a world of mergers, buyouts, downsizing, upsizing, and bankruptcy. That's why it's more important than ever to be at the top of your game and always ready to show just how valuable you are.

If the current statistics hold true, you will be interviewing quite often, and if nothing else, you will be looking at receiving a raise and possible promotion within your current company. That's why it has become increasingly important to be able to demonstrate your experience and knowledge in a way that sets you apart as the top candidate.

The issue at hand is not whether you're able to verbalize your accomplishments and experiences, although that may be part of it. More importantly, it's your ability to bring your experiences and accomplishments to life so that the person you're interviewing with understands and sees your true worth. In my experience, and through talking with managers and directors of many companies, very few people are able to articulate their importance and value to a company in such a way as to leave a positive impression that is lasting. You may do things well, and you may even do many things great, but are you able to convey those so that others understand just how great they are? This is where the importance of being able to promote, package, market, and communicate your experiences and accomplishments comes into play.

By the end of this book you will have created a personal Success Portfolio highlighting your accomplishments and experiences. This portfolio will be the platform for all of your future interviews and/or reviews. Have you ever heard the saying "out of sight, out of mind"? Your Success Portfolio will keep you at the front of the interviewer's memory after the interview is over and you have left. It continues to impress, even in your absence. In later chapters we will get into creating your binder, but for now let's focus on why it is so important to stand out among the rest.

According to the U.S. Department of Labor's Bureau of Labor Statistics Report dated June 2006, there are 116.4 million people employed full time with an additional 21 million employed part time. There are also approximately 9 million college students in their third year or higher, including graduate school. You now add in the over 4.6 million jobs that have been lost since 2008 and there is a lot of competition going for the same positions. Why do I share this data with you? Simple: you must first understand how many people are vying for the same job you want. You must also understand that if you are not able to show your value to a company, there are plenty of other people ready to step in and take your place. These figures are not intended to scare or alarm you, but rather to put things in perspective. It is time for you to step out from the crowd, see the possibilities that lie in front of you, and take action. Don't wait for others to ask what you bring to the table; be bold and show them!

> *"When you see the word impossible you should always*
> *see I'm Possible."*
> **-James Malinchak**

By the time you finish reading this book, you will be equipped to boldly step out from the crowd and to let your achievements help to confidently speak for you. Although this system may not get you in the corner office or guarantee a pay increase of 25% by tomorrow, it will put you on the right track to help realizing your dreams. You will have to do work in the process, but there is nothing I will be sharing that I have not done myself. Everything here is within your reach, and I firmly believe in you and your abilities.

Remember, you only need to take one step at a time, and before you know it you will be ready to handle any scenario that comes your way. So, turn the page and let's get started!

"Champions aren't made in the gyms.
Champions are made from something they have deep inside them –
a desire, a dream, a vision."
-Muhammad Ali

3

Organization: Creating Files for Your Accomplishments

"First comes thought; then organization of that thought,
into ideas and plans; then transformation of those plans into reality.
The beginning, as you will observe, is in your imagination."
-Napoleon Hill

Organization is a scary word for many people; in fact, some may say that there is no way they will ever be organized with everything that goes on in their day-to-day lives. This is something that you will have to get over, because although organization is not easy, it can be done. Being able to sort out the important from the unimportant is a critical first step.

When you are getting ready for an interview or a future review or promotion will you be able to pull up information on your past work and accomplishments to help you prepare? Are you ready to answer any questions you may be asked and support your answer with written facts? For most people, the answer is no.

Today you will start a new system that will help you make the most of your time. It will take some effort and time upfront, but in the end it will be worth it. Have you ever heard the expression that "anything worthwhile takes time"? I'm not sure who originally said it, but it's very true. Many times we expect to have things brought to us on a silver platter as if they can just magically appear. But if you wait long enough for that silver platter, reality will soon set in and you'll realize that's not how things work.

Let's say you have a goal of getting your first job out of college and moving up the corporate ladder. If you want that to become a reality, you have to work for it. You will need to put in the time it takes to understand your position and the new position. You will have needed to prove yourself through your work habits, your determination, and your abilities, just to name a few. It will take work to reach the next level, but if that's your goal, it's worth it. The same holds true for creating your Success Portfolio. It will take some work in the beginning, but the rewards will be great.

Let's start with the basics: a filing system. This filing system can be done on the computer or through actual paper files. I know it's hard to believe for many of you, but yes, many people still use paper files, including myself. I keep as much as I can on my computer, but I also keep copies of many documents in my paper filing system. I would suggest that if you tend to keep everything on your computer that you also make room for some paper filing and that you back up your documents. The rationale for maintaining paper files is because not all important documents or correspondence that you may need to access later are in electronic form.

First, let's look at the paper filing method. In order to set up your filing drawer, you will need hanging file folders and/or manila file folders, depending on the type of filing cabinet you purchase or may already have. You will then need tabs for the hanging folders or simply a marking pen for the manila folders; you can't get much easier than that.

At this point you are ready to start brainstorming. I want you to put yourself in the hot seat and imagine you are sitting across from your future manager for a review or that you are sitting at a table across from a couple of people who are interviewing you for a new job. What things do you want to make sure you mention about yourself before you leave that room? What accomplishments are you most proud of? What experiences set you apart? What have you done while in college that really makes you stand out? What have others said about you or your work that makes you proud? Think of those things and start to list them out on a piece of paper.

Some examples that come to mind may be your résumé, solutions you have provided for customers or your company if you worked a part time job while in school; training or certifications you have completed or received; training that you may have provided to others; feedback from your peers, teachers, coworkers, customers, manager, and/or others; awards received; events you helped coordinate such as an alumni dinner; clubs you were a part of, projects you led or worked on for a class, sports activities, leadership rolls, helping raise money for the school, fraternity, sorority participation, special projects for a class, your GPA; references, and the list goes on. These will be the headings for your folders.

You will begin to put each topic on a different folder. Be ready to make new folders in the coming months, because you will think of new topics.

Now, as you have examples of your work that fit into these areas, you will want to print a copy of each document you thought of and put it in the appropriate file folder to use later. It's always good to have multiple copies of certain documents to make sure you are covered. The same filing system should be created on your computer. Create a folder titled "My Success Portfolio" or something similar. Then create sub-files in your "My Success Portfolio" file and title them as you titled the paper files. When you have information come to you on your computer in the way of documents, e-mails, etc., you can save it in the appropriate folder. As you create different items, you will want to save a copy in these folders also. In the future it may be a copy of a budget you put together, a proposal to a customer that won you the business, letters you send to your customers that show how well you communicate, thank-you notes from customers, commendation/appreciation letters, goal-setting worksheets, or strategies you have put in place.

By taking the time upfront, you will be ready to gather all your information when needed. It's also a good idea to go through your files, both on the computer and in paper format to see where you may be lacking. If you find that you don't have anything within a certain area, you can start working on gathering data for that given item.

The bottom line is that you want to be able to locate all the information you will need to create your portfolio and to benefit you in future interviews or reviews as quickly and easily as possible. By keeping your filing system current, you will be ready for anything that comes your way.

You are now on your way to creating a very easy and well-planed system to better prepare yourself for future raises, promotions, and interviews. If only organizing the rest of your life were this easy!

4

Your Résumé and Cover Letter:
The Importance of Making Them Great

"Talent is a gift, but character is a choice."
-John C. Maxwell

This chapter is not about going over the principles of putting together a great résumé and cover letter; it seems there are enough books on that topic to circle the earth. No, this chapter will simply state the obvious, but sometimes the obvious is often overlooked. A clear, concise résumé and cover letter that grabs the interest of those reading it should be your goal. Take advantage of the career department at your school. They have countless books and examples of great résumés.

At the end of this chapter I have included a few examples of résumés and a couple of cover letters. Some of these are for individuals that have been working for some time which will be a great help when you are going for future promotions. Behind each résumé I have broken out possible sections you could create in your Success Portfolio based on the résumé. This will help you see how to break out your experiences based on your résumé to create a great Success Portfolio. These samples may not necessarily be the best format for your situation; however, they do include characteristics to highlight the candidate's strengths.

Your résumé should bring a detailed summary of your work history, including your work, education, and achievements. Even though you are just getting out of school, you still must have a résumé.

Remember, a résumé is not the time for you to write a full-length autobiography; it is an opportunity to highlight your accomplishments and make them come alive for the reader. You want to use action and power words that really describe your ability and accomplishments.

In the "objective" part of your résumé, be specific. I have read more résumés than I care to think of in which the person requesting the position never mentioned the position they were going for. People send general résumés that they probably send to hundreds of other companies for various positions, and it shows. You want to make each résumé specific to the job and company for which you are applying. Yes, this will take extra time, but it also sets your résumé apart from 95% of all the other candidates applying for a certain position.

When listing out your experiences, match your experience with the qualifications the employer is looking for as much as possible. In the employer's job description and qualifications, there will generally be a list of specific things for which the company is looking. As much as you can, show through your experience that you have the qualities they want. If you have had a part time job you will list your past jobs starting with the most current and then work back from there.

Use power words as much as possible when describing your experience; you want the potential employer to see action in your words.

Here is a short list of power words:

Accomplished, achieved, advised, awarded, bought, caused, changed, completed, conducted, consolidated, coordinated, created, delegated, demonstrated, designed, developed, doubled, earned, effected, enlarged, executed, focused, formulated, generated, handled, identified, implemented, improved, influenced, instructed, invented, launched, led, made, managed, motivated, negotiated, organized, oversaw, participated, persuaded, planned, presented, programmed, promoted, published, purchased, qualified, raised, ranked, received, reduced, represented, saved, selected, set up, sold, solved, sparked, streamlined, strengthened, succeeded, supervised, tackled, taught, tested, traded, transformed, tripled, uncovered, upgraded, won.

There's one thing that I must mention before going any further: be yourself and don't put down things that are not true, even if it's just stretching the truth a little. You may be thinking, "It's not a big deal if I put down some experiences or accomplishments that are not exactly true." You could not be more wrong. What happens when you are asked to back them up? When we pretend to be someone we are not, we only build a wall between ourselves and others and hope that they never find out the truth. I have hired people when they had less experience than other candidates because they were upfront about it and demonstrated an eager attitude to learn. It's exhausting having to keep up a false front once you start down a path of not being yourself. Trust is something that is very hard to get back once you cross the line of not telling the truth, no matter how small or insignificant the lie may seem at the time. In most cases, the résumé is your first impression; it's important that you make it real and make it count.

Next time you're tempted to tell someone a lie because you don't think the truth is good enough, remember what Mark Batterson says in his book, *In a Pit with a Lion on a Snowy Day:* "I'd rather be disliked for who I am than liked for who I'm not."

Now let's look at your cover letter. It should be well thought out, descriptive and also specific to the position for which you are applying. What I mean by this is that you should take the extra time to list out the position you are applying for in the body of the cover letter, along with a brief description of your qualifications. Think of your cover letter as a teaser to get the person or persons interested in learning more about you. Because of this, you don't want to repeat word for word your résumé within the cover letter. Use the cover letter as a way of hitting the highlights and saying it in a fresh way. You want to be able to show how you meet and exceed the qualifications of the job as described in the job posting. You should pick the top two or three items they are looking for in a candidate listed in the job posting and share how you would be a great fit. Think of the cover letter as your introduction. You should show your excitement for the position through your use of words. This is your chance to wow them and make them want to find out more about you.

You should try to keep the cover letter to one page and address it to a specific person whenever possible. If you don't have a name, try calling the company for which you are applying and ask the receptionist for the name of the person in charge of hiring for this position. If you are put in touch with the actual person in charge of hiring for this position, simply introduce yourself, let him or her know that you are going to be applying for the position (tell the position name in case he or she is doing the hiring for multiple positions), and ask to whom you could address your application for employment. As a last resort, if you are not able to find out a specific name, simply address your cover letter to "Sir or Madam."

For more information on creating the best cover letter and résumé, I would suggest the following books. These are just a few of the many that are available, but these are ones that I have found to be most useful.

- Adams Media, *Résumé Almanac Second Edition*
- Adams Media, *Job Interview Almanac*
- Bob Adams, *The Everything Job Interview Book*
- Martin Yate, *Résumés that Knock 'em Dead*
- Martin Yate, *Cover Letters that Knock 'em Dead*
- Martin Yate, *The Ultimate Job Search Guide (Knock 'em Dead)*

Sample Résumé 1

John Campbell

2468 S. Main Street   *City, State Zip Code*   *Phone (555) 123-4567*
e-mail@address.com

Objective: To gain a position in sales with HY-HO Inc., where my drive, determination, enthusiasm, and desire to succeed would be utilized to make an immediate impact in helping HY-HO Inc. achieve its goal of being the best widget company.

Summary: Highly motivated and excellent communicator with a passion to succeed. While at the university I took every opportunity to learn and put into practice my leadership and selling skills. My experience in sales and negotiation served me well in raising over $20,000 for the athletic association in one semester and achieving 40% growth as a Sales/Shift Manager. I managed a team of four while working for a local company where I learned the importance of listening, relationship building, people skills, and the art of delegation all while in school as a full-time student.

Experience: **Coffee House, Blacksburg**, VA   2004-April 2006
Sales/Shift Manager

Led a team of four in achieving dramatic growth in sales where we experienced a 40% growth rate in new customers.

- ◆ Responsible for all training for my team
- ◆ Set goals and budget
- ◆ Increased sales
- ◆ Developed a Customer Appreciation Plan
- ◆ Provided exceptional customer service

University Athletic Association, Blacksburg, VA   2005-2006

Strategically raised $20,000 to aid in building a new athletic facility that would benefit students. As a volunteer I was able to take on a leadership role in helping raise money and share a vision for the future in which others wanted to take an active role.

Honors, Leadership Roles, and Activities:

- ◆ Outstanding Achievement Award in Sales
- ◆ Pledge Director for Local Chapter of Fraternity (list fraternity name)
- ◆ Participated in Numerous Intramural Sports

Education: Virginia Polytechnic Institute and State University, Blacksburg, VA   April 2006
Business Administration

References available upon request

Success Portfolio Sections for Sample Résumé 1

The following are examples of sections you could have in your Success Portfolio based on Sample Résumé 1. Also, within each section are listed possible examples that you could put in your Success Portfolio to demonstrate your experience in that area.

- *Résumé*

- *Sales Results*
    - Include reports that show your sales results, graphs that show your results, and other forms of documentation that would support your results. In sample résumé 1 it shows a 40% growth in new customers; you will need to provide numbers, charts, etc. to support that figure or show how you determined that percentage.

- *Fundraising*
    - Include examples of how you raised money. In sample résumé 1 it states that $20,000 was raised in one semester. How was that achieved? Was it through phone calls, door to door campaigns, flyers? If flyers were used, include a copy of the flyer. Let them know that you don't take no for an answer and you don't stop till you reach your goal.

- *Leadership*
    - This could include examples of when you took the lead on a special project for a class or job that was very successful. It could be an example of when you were a captain or co captain while on a team and what you did while in that role. The responsibility you had while captain or co captain and what you learned from that experience. It could be coaching forms you used when working with someone on your team while at the Coffee House. Look for examples that really show off your skills in being a leader.

- *Communication*
  - Include examples of how you communicate with employees, your team, and other professionals. You could print a copy of e-mails you send out that show your communication style in keeping everyone informed.

- *Awards/Honors*
  - Provide examples of awards by way of copies of an award given, certificates, plaques, etc.

- *Offices Held*
  - In sample résumé 1 it gives the example of being Pledge Director for the local fraternity. Do you have any records that show that? You could share the role you played and all that was involved in holding this position, the responsibility that you had, and how you demonstrated your leadership qualities.

- *Activities and Clubs*
  - Include records of any activities you participated in while in school. Maybe you played intramural sports, gave campus tours, participated in clubs, or any number of other items.

Sample Résumé 2

Tim Johnson
1155 Somewhere Street
City, State Zip Code
Telephone (555) 123-4567 ~ Cell (555) 321-7654
e-mail@address.com

Objective: To obtain a position in sales with (list company name) in which I can bring together my experience in public speaking and influencing others along with a solid understanding of business leadership and relationship building to help (list company name) achieve its goals.

Education: ***Masters of Business Administration***, *Date obtained*
College/University Name, City, State
GPA: 3.2 (optional)

Bachelor of Business Administration, *Date obtained*
Minor in Marketing
College/University Name, City, State

Summary: Excellent communicator, especially skilled at building effective, productive working relationships with clients and staff. More than nine years of sales and sales management experience with a track record of producing exceptional results. Proven leadership and experience in working with others in a team environment. Able to build cohesiveness so the objective can be obtained in a quick and effective manner through innovative solutions. A skilled negotiator with strong management, sales, and marketing background.

Professional Experience: (start with most recent)
Job Title
Name of Company, City, State
Date Started with Company – Date left company or position

Job Description:
Provided inspirational leadership and strategic direction to the sales force in order to achieve 125% to goal based on performance objectives. Worked with key customers to form a solid relationship built on trust. Managed a district with overall sales of more than $3.5 million.

Major Responsibilities:
♦ **Develop People:**
 o Drove business by providing ongoing counsel to a team of ten Sales Specialists; provided them with individual coaching, feedback, and inspiration; helped Sales Specialists develop success in current role and for future growth.
♦ **Ensure Commitment:**
 o Built commitment for the shared vision by facilitating team communication, morale, and effectiveness. As a role model, I inspired trust and commitment.
♦ **Influence Others:**
 o Identified and adjusted to the different needs of key stakeholders. Acted as a liaison between the sales force and other cross-functional areas, persuading, convincing, and motivating a targeted audience through collaboration and direct or indirect influence. Appealed to others' underlying sources of motivation and developed a shared sense of responsibility for ultimate results.
♦ **Deliver Results:**
 o Set ambitious goals and exceeded them by 125% by identifying strategic business opportunities and then delivering the end result. Accountable for achieving standards of excellence set by myself and (list company name).

Job Title
Name of Company, City, State
Date Started with Company – Date left company

Major Responsibilities:
♦ Responsible for increased access for Sales Representatives across selling teams in more than 75 accounts by use of innovative patient and medical solutions customized for each account.
♦ Worked with the district team to reinforce customer planning, allocation of resources and integration of plans.

Job Title
Name of Company, City, State
Date Started with Company – Date left company

Major Responsibilities:
♦ Directly influenced prescribing habits and preferences of more than 100 physicians and other key advocates.
♦ Provided customized solutions and developed and leveraged relationships with key doctors to be a partner in their practice.

Awards
Top Sales Producer 2006
Training Champion 2005
Most Improved Performance 2005

References available upon request

Success Portfolio Sections for Sample Résumé 2

The following are examples of sections you could have in your Success Binder, based on Sample Résumé 2. Also, within each section are possible examples that you could put in your Success Binder to demonstrate your experience in that area.

- *Cover Letter*

- *Résumé*

- *Sales Results*
  - Include reports that show your sales results, graphs that show your results, and other forms of documentation that would support your results. In sample résumé 2 it shows a 125% to goal on performance objectives, so you will need to provide numbers, charts, etc. to support that figure. That way, when your interviewers ask you to share how you achieved those numbers, you have documentation supporting your achievement. You would then have them turn in your success binder to this example. Now you are ready to show them the steps you took to achieve this goal. *You have not just answered their question, but you have aced their question and set yourself apart as a top candidate.*

- *Leadership*
  - Include examples of leadership. This could be examples of when you took the lead on a project that was very successful. It could be coaching forms you used when working with someone on your team or within the company. Look for examples that really show off your skills in being a leader.

- *Coaching* (could be combined with Leadership)
  - This could be coaching or feedback forms on your performance by your manager or on people to whom you have given coaching or feedback. If they are based on your performance, it shows how you have done in the eyes of your manager, and it also gives you a great chance to talk about areas that were seen as opportunities to improve. You can then share what you did to improve in an area and how that has helped you in your position. These are great to use if asked a question on how you handle criticism. You are able to share an example and then have them turn to this section of your Success Binder and show where the remarks were made and what you did to turn that situation around and what steps you took to improve in that area.

- *Goal Planning*
  - Include examples of how you planned out the steps to achieve the goals the company had set for you or goals that you set for yourself above and beyond the company's goals. Break it out so you can show your thought process by having the end goal at the top of the page with the action steps taken to reach that goal listed below.

- *Performance Reviews*
  - You should include past performance reviews given to you by your manager, director, etc. This brings credibility to how your work was viewed. It shows your areas of strength and those areas where you can improve. This will also give you the opportunity to address any area that may have been an area for improvement. You can go into detail on the steps you took to gain expertise in that area. This shows your ability to take direction and then act upon it.

- *Special Projects*
  - Include examples of any projects that really demonstrate your abilities. These are great examples to use when asked questions such as, "Tell me about a time when you had to work on a team or by yourself to complete a job with a deadline" or, "Tell me about a time when you had to work with a difficult customer on a project" or, "What accomplishment are you most proud of in your current position?"

- *Development Plan*
  - In this section you could include your goals for the future. Many companies now have their employees put together a development plan for where they want to go in the company and the steps it will take to get there. If you have not completed one of these with your company, you should complete one on your own. List out your goals for the next year, three years, five years, and beyond. Next, list out the steps needed to achieve each goal in that timeline.

Sample Résumé 3

Mary Smith
1155 Somewhere Street
City, State, Zip Code
Telephone (555) 123-4567 ~ Cell (555) 321-7654
e-mail@address.com

Objective: To acquire a position in Human Resource Management with XYZ Company where my management, sales, and recruiting talents can be utilized to improve operations and ultimately help XYZ Company achieve its goals.

Summary: Over twelve years of human resources experience; solid leadership skills combined with a strong work ethic, drive, and determination have produced extraordinary results; experience in leading a team at multiple-site locations.

Experience: **ABC CORPORATION**, Dallas, TX   1998-Present
Human Resources Manager

Responsible for the training, recruiting, and managing of a staff of eight. Work with over 200 employees at the primary site in all areas of their work benefits. Set up interviews, selection process, creation of interview questioners, and all aspects of hiring for ABC Corporation.

- Achieved less than 2% turnover year over year
- Trained three new managers due to expansion in the past six months
- Improved communication between employees and management by developing a new and exciting communication platform

Additional Responsibilities:
- Supervise eight other site locations
- Counsel
- Leadership trainer for the sales team totaling over 350 employees
- Create and manage annual budget

KLM EXECUTIVES, Chicago, IL   1994-1998
Recruiting company for Fortune 500 companies
Recruiting Manager for Key Accounts

As Recruiting Manager, I worked with fifteen key accounts that made up the top 4% of KLM Executives revenue. I was responsible for the hiring of management-level employees and above to include, but not limited to, Senior Managers, Directors, and Regional Directors.

Eductaion: University of Richmond, VA
B.S. Public Relations, 1994
Minor in Marketing

References: Available upon request

Success Binder Sections for Sample Résumé 3

The following are example sections you could have, based on Sample Résumé 3. Also, within each section are possible examples that you could put in your Success Binder to demonstrate your experience in that area.

- *Cover Letter*

- *Résumé*

- *Training*
  - Include examples of how you trained people. Any items you created to aid in the process. What types of training did you do, and/or what types of training did you take?

- *Recruiting*
  - Include steps you took in recruiting. Show examples of ways you creatively recruited. What did the process look like? How many steps were there and what role did you play in each?

- *Interviewing*
  - Include examples of questions you would ask, and be prepared to tell them why you would ask those questions. Did you create any documentation that helped in the interview process that was used? If so, include that here.

- *Goals*
  - Include examples of how you planned out the steps to achieve the goals the company had set for you or goals that you set for yourself above and beyond the company's goals. Break it out so you can show your thought process by having the end goal at the top of the page with the action steps taken to reach that goal below.

- *Achievements*
  - Include special achievements that you are most proud of and that really set you apart. In Sample Résumé 2 it states that this person "Achieved less than 2% turnover year over year." This person should include whether she received any recognition for this in the way of a certificate, plaque, letter, or awards. If so, include that in this section. Also, how was such a low turnover rate achieved?

- *Communication*

  Include examples of how you communicate with employees, your team, and other people in a professional environment. You could print a copy of e-mails you send out that show your communication style in keeping everyone informed. It could be in the form of a newsletter you may put together or are responsible for.

- *Development Plan*

  In this section you could include your goals for the future. Many companies now have their employees put together a development plan/roadmap for where they want to go in the company and the steps it will take to get there. If you have not completed one of these with your company you should complete one on your own. List out your goals for the next year, three years, five years, and beyond. Next, list out the steps needed to achieve each goal in that timeline.

Sample Cover Letter 1

(Your Address)
5555 Maple Lane
Atlanta, GA 22222
(555) 555-5555 (h)
(333) 333-3333 (c)

August 30, 2010

Ms. Jane Carpenter
Director of Sales
Widgets International
One Widget Drive
Houston, TX 75310

Dear Ms. Carpenter:

I am excited to submit my résumé for your review for the position of Sales Representative with Widget International. I bring enthusiasm, drive, determination, and a never-take-no-for-an-answer attitude that would serve me well in being an immediate contributor to Widget International. I believe I have the qualifications for your serious consideration and would appreciate the opportunity to demonstrate this through a personal interview.

My experience in sales and managing as the Sales/Shift Manager while at the Coffee House has prepared me to be a top producer on your team. Also, while going to school full time, I strategically raised $20,000 for our athletic department. This was done through my dynamic sales and relationship-building skills. I have held numerous roles in organizations while attending Virginia Polytechnic Institute and State University and had the opportunity to hone my leadership skills. This, along with my sales experience and education, make me a great fit for Widgets International.

I possess strong written and verbal communication skills and a dynamic presentation/public speaking style. Let me also note that one of my greatest strengths is my ability to build and cultivate strong relationships. I have the talent and skills needed to immediately make a positive impact on the bottom line and I am ready to bring my experience and excitement to work for you.

I am confident in my ability to meet and exceed your expectations for this position and look forward to meeting with you for a personal interview. I will follow up in a week to verify the receipt of my application and answer any questions you may have.

Sincerely,

John Campbell

John Campbell

Sample Cover Letter 2

55555 Main Street
Richmond, VA 22222
(555) 555-5555 (h)
(333) 333-3333 (c)

August 30, 2010

Mr. Mark Fuller
Vice President of Stewardship Development
ABC International
P.O. Box 12345
Boston, MA 43434

Dear Mr. Fuller:

I am excited to submit my résumé for your review for the position of Regional Director of Stewardship Development with ABC International and know my experience and dedication would serve you well. I believe I have the qualifications for your serious consideration and would appreciate the opportunity to demonstrate this through a personal interview.

My experience in developing and sustaining dynamic relationships would prove invaluable in raising funds from existing donors and new prospects, so the mission of ABC International would be achieved. I have a solid understanding of how Fortune 500 corporations work through my experience as a Regional Director and as a Fundraising Manager. This, along with my strong business background and education, makes me a great fit for ABC International.

I possess strong written and verbal communication skills and a dynamic presentation/public speaking style. Let me also note that one of my greatest strengths is my ability to build and cultivate strong relationships. I have a background in sales and sales management through which I used my abilities to influence others and solicit their business with great results, all built on trust.

I am confident in my ability to meet and exceed your expectations for this position and look forward to meeting with you for a personal interview. I will follow up in a week to verify the receipt of my application and answer any questions you may have.

Sincerely,

Steve Thompson

Steve Thompson

5

The Sections of Your Success Portfolio

"To succeed, jump as quickly at opportunities as you do at conclusions."
-Benjamin Franklin

In this chapter we will look at the different sections you could have in your Success Portfolio and go into detail for each one. Specifically, we will cover examples of items that you can include in each section and begin the process of pulling everything together. These are by no means the only sections you can have. This is only an outline to help you get started. You may have specific sections that pertain to your life and job experience that are not listed here. A word of caution: don't overload your portfolio with too many sections; you want it to be easy for the person you're sharing it with to read and understand. The ideal number of sections would be between five and ten. This is just an ideal, but it does not mean you can't go under or over either of these. The more sections you create, the better prepared you must be. If you have twelve or fifteen sections, for example, you are going to have a harder time remembering all the examples you have and where to turn when you want to share one of them. Keep it simple and easy for you to use and for the person to follow. The great thing about this is that you're the author, so make it your own.

I have included examples that are both specific to students in college and examples that you may have once you begin working. This will help you see opportunities for you to use in getting future promotions and even larger raises. Even the sections that don't seem to fit your situation now are good to read over because in may help you remember an experience you had forgotten.

Section Examples

Cover Page: This is simply a page with your name, address, contact numbers, and e-mail. You want to put your name on the upper part of the page, centered and enlarged so that it stands out. Put the remaining information below it, about three-quarters of the way down the page. If you put your binder together with a clear front cover, which is what I would recommend, the cover page with your name and contact information is what people will see.

Cover Letter: You may want to include a copy of the cover letter you sent in with your résumé. If you do include your cover letter, I would suggest putting it directly after your cover page as your first tab. Make sure you have saved all the cover letters you have done, and I would suggest you save them under the name of the company. You don't want to use a cover letter that has the name of another company on it! Make sure you read over it before including it. In many cases when you are interviewing, it will be with a number of people. Only one may have seen your cover letter where you highlight all your skills and experiences. By including it at the beginning of your Success Portfolio, the others that are now interviewing you have the opportunity to read over that information.

Résumé: The next tab after your cover letter should be your résumé, *because* it's the foundation on which the rest of your work is based. Even though you want to give the person you are meeting with a copy of your résumé, always include another copy in the front of your binder. It is always good to include your résumé for an interview, but if you are just using this to aid you in getting a larger pay increase at an upcoming review, the résumé may not be needed; however, by keeping your résumé updated at all times, you are prepared for whatever comes your way. It also might remind your current manager just how good of an employee you are, how much you do, and how valuable you are to the company.

Undergrad/Graduate GPA(optional): This is where you put a copy of your transcript or diploma. Your GPA is a tool employers look to for a measure of your commitment and focus. This does not mean you must have a great GPA to get a job; I'm a testament to that. It *does* show that you care enough not to hide anything. A good rule of thumb is to not include your GPA if it's below 2.0, because that may draw unnecessary attention. Keep in mind that if your GPA was not stellar you will want to make sure you have solid examples to show how you excelled in other areas.

Leadership: Include examples of when you took the lead on a project or a team. Have you managed others or been responsible for how a project turned out? Were you a team captain? Put items in this section that substantiates your leadership skills. Do you have an example of when you took the lead and it was a great success? Look for items that make your leadership experience stand out and make people take notice. An example of this could be an e-mail, note, or a letter you received from your teacher, coach, manager or coworker commending you on your leadership work. It could also be a copy of a business plan you put together for a given project where you took the lead or any awards you received.

Internship: If you worked as an intern, list that information in this section. During that time, were there any special projects you worked on, any notes you were given, or any learning experiences that really stand out? Did you have a review of your work? If so, include that information in this section.

Events/Activities: Maybe you helped organize an alumni dinner. Share all that went into such an event like getting volunteers, coordinating with different campus departments, setting up the food and decorations. What was your role and what did you learn? How did what you learned doing this prepare you for the position or positions you will be interviewing for?

Did you help organize an event or activity for a class you took, for a fraternity or sorority, for a fundraising event for the sports department? You want to be able to take what you leaned doing the event and make it translate into a real world example that will make people interviewing you take notice. If you helped with marketing the event turn that into how you would be able to market for the company. What type of success did the event have and show how the marketing impacted that success. How you understood the audience and that allowed you to focus your efforts on things that drew people to the event. Be ready to share what those things were that you did.

Maybe you were in charge of delegating multiple tasks to others and making sure things got done. Show how your experience in working as a team leader has prepared you for success in the corporate world. You understand what it takes to bring people together to achieve a common goal. You are able to effectively delegate in a manner that makes people excited to be a part of what's going on and they want to give it 110%.

You would include information on this event in your Success Portfolio. It could be a flyer on the event. It could be statistics showing how much money was raised and a brief summary of what you did to contribute to making the event a success. Make it come alive so the people you will be meeting with can see and understand how you have taken what you learned in this example and are ready to apply it to the position you are interviewing for.

Business Plans: You can put together a plan on how you're going about getting a job—what you have done up to this point to prepare yourself to interview, resources you used, ways you researched the company you are interviewing with, other ways you prepared, and what your ultimate goal is. This shows you are able to plan, put that plan into action, and that you have a clear goal in mind.

In the future when you are going for a promotion or a position at another company you would include a business plan on how you're doing in your current position, what your goals are, and how you're going to reach those goals. It's an opportunity for you to share past goals, what strategy or strategies you put in place, and the tactics you used to achieve them. By including this, it shows your ability to understand your business, how it affects the overall company, and your ability to plan and strategize for the future.

It could also be a business plan you put together on winning a new customer or saving the company money.

Communication: How do you communicate? What methods work best for you? In this section you want to give examples of your communication style. It could be as simple as copies of a newsletter you put together for an event. Are you someone that likes to send personal note cards to people letting them know what a great job they have done or thanking customers for their business? If so include a couple of examples by photocopying a note you sent to someone. You may send out weekly e-mails giving updates for the week ahead; this is a great thing to print out and include in your portfolio. The point is that you want to show how you communicate with others. The more examples you can give that show diversity the better. Not everyone responds to e-mails, so it's great if you can show multiple styles of communicating. This shows that you are able to adapt and understand that each person responds differently to different ways of communication. If you are always using the same style to communicate such as e-mail, maybe you need to shake things up a bit and try other ways to communicate, such as memos, notes, newsletters, etc.

Fundraising: Think of examples of how you have raised money. Maybe you helped through a phone-a-thon where you made phone calls to perspective donors. Maybe you created flyers that were distributed to prospects. Maybe you went door to door collecting donations. All of these are great examples to include. How much money did you raise? What was the reason for the fundraising and did you or the school achieve its goal? How did you use your communicate skills to get people to give money? You may have been responsible for a national campaign that was given the task of collecting millions of dollars. In all of these examples there are opportunities to show your experience in this area. If your experience is via the phone, include examples of questions you would ask and the dialogue you would have with people on the phone. If you created flyers include a copy of the flyer. You may be an expert at networking with people. If so, how do you make contact with them and share the needs of your company, organization etc.

As you move on in your career you may be responsible for a large fundraising campaign. You will want to provide greater detail because of all the different rolls you played. You could provide an outline of how you strategized on the different ways to raise money. Maybe you put together a dinner or golf tournament to help raise the funds. In these cases you would include an outline of all the responsibilities you had and how you prioritized them in order to make the event a great success.

Remember, you want to be able to walk the interviewer through your example. Start at the beginning, sharing your thought process and what went into starting the project, and then move them along to how you pulled it all together. Maybe you delegated many roles to other people. You would want to include that here to show how you are also able to lead. You would end by showing the people the result of all your hard work. The greater the dollar amount you have raised the more important it is to include that in your examples. Let the people see the responsibility you had.

Volunteerism: Do you have examples of areas where you have volunteered? Have you given of your time to help others out in any way? This helps provide a rounded picture of who you are. Maybe you got a certificate for helping out or you may have helped lead in a certain way. This can be as easy as listing out examples of how you have volunteered along with a little background on each. Don't take this opportunity to spend a lot of time sharing about your passions.

Remember, you want to get across the main points, show them you're the right person for the position or that you are deserving of a greater pay increase without lecturing them on what gets you excited. We can get carried away sometimes when we begin talking about our passions. When this happens it can quickly turn a person off and they begin to shut down and stop listening. Hit the main points and turn it back to them by asking a simple question such as, "As you can see, I am very passionate and committed to helping out and getting the task at hand done. Are these qualities you look for in a person?"

Sports: This is for those who played organized sports or maybe you helped start a new intramural sports group at school. Include in this section items around the sport or sports you played that really set you apart—scholarships awarded, playing time, awards received. Share what skills you learned from this experience such as leadership and how it helped make you a better person and will make you a great fit for a given position.

Success Stories: Do you have a success story that really shows off your skills and abilities that pertain to the position you are going for or the raise you are going after in your current position? Give a little background on the story, what you did in preparing, how you went about completing the work needed to be done and the outcome. This is not the time to write a book, but a brief outline of the story, which would allow the interviewer or person you are meeting with (if it's for a raise) to get know just enough to make him want to hear more. This would then give you the opportunity to elaborate on it more. You want to peak the person's interest to want to hear more. As an example, the employer may see on your résumé where you stated, "Led a team of eight to raise $15,000 for charity." He may ask you to tell him how you did this and what happened. This would be the time when you would have him turn to this tab and walk him through your experience in a brief and concise manner.

Professional Feedback: Maybe you have gotten feedback from a professor or advisor on a project you completed. It could be feedback from others within the college or from a manager if you worked while going to school. These are those notes, e-mails, or letters you may have received on past work or accomplishments. You want to copy these and include them so you can show how others feel about your work and the effort and support you give. These can be as simple as an e-mail saying, "Great job!" or a note sharing how you really helped out on a special project.

Special Projects: List special projects you have been involved in and the outcome. If you have any documentation, include that in this section. Again, it brings validity.

Awards: You may have awards you are proud of that show your abilities and accomplishments. If they are in the form of certificates, you want to make a clean photocopy and include them in this section. If they are plaques, you can try to photocopy and include them; if they will not clearly copy, create a printed list of all your awards.

Offices Held: You may be an active member in a school club or you have held an office in the local community back home. These experiences are all valuable because they show leadership ability. These could include roles such as class president, Greek life positions, sports leadership roles, board positions in organizations, serving as a director, secretary, etc.

References: This is where you would list out people whom you have already spoken with about being a reference for you. Because these people will be contacted to gather information on you, make sure you talk with them prior to including them on this list. Usually references are asked how they know you, how they see you as a leader, about your work ethic, what history they have with you, what strengths they see you as having, what weaknesses they see you as having, and whether they recommend you for this position.

When listing a person as a reference, you want to include the person's name, title, place of employment, address, phone number, and e-mail address. A reference could be a teacher, your current manager if working, people you have worked for in the past during the summer, or a pastor, to name a few. You want to include references that bring credibility to your experience and that have a working knowledge of you. Now is not the time to include your best friend unless they happen to also be working with you and can offer solid examples of your experience.

You can also include letters of recommendation that people have written about you in this section. If you have someone that is highly thought of in your profession that has written a recommendation for you, by all means include that here and make a point of bringing it to the interviewer's attention.

Mentoring: Have you ever been a mentor for someone? List what you did when working with this person. This demonstrates that you are someone to whom others to look for information and guidance. You are seen as a leader that others respect and want to learn from.

Teaming: What teams were you on and did you have a leadership role. It could be as simple as being on a team for a class project. This area gives you a lot of things you can discuss during an interview. Many times people will ask you to share a time you were on a team and there were issues between the different team members. How did you handle the situation and what was the outcome. You would be able to take them to this section, show them the team you were on and a copy or outline of what you team accomplished. You could then discuss the issue that arose and the role you took in getting it corrected. (You can find additional information on how to answer this question in chapter 6, Situational Planning.)

Development: What have you done to develop yourself so you are ready for this job? Sure you have been in school for 4 years or so but what else have you done? What steps have you taken to set yourself apart from others through continued education, seminars taken, or online courses that would relate to what you are going to be interviewing for? If you have not done anything like this now is the time! Look for opportunities on the internet to learn more about the area you want to work in. Are there online classes you can take to provide you greater in site and that would set you apart from others?

In the future, many companies have their employees complete a development plan once a year. In this plan you list out your short-term goals, within the next one or two years, and also your long-term goals, within the next three to five years. If you are asked to complete a plan such as this you could include a copy of that plan in this section for future raises or promotions. Typically you list out your goals within the company such as a job promotion or going from an account manager to senior account manager. Maybe you have set as a short-term goal to be the rookie of the year. Many times the person interviewing you will want to have you share the steps you are taking to achieve the goals set in the development plan, so be prepared to share this information.

Training/Development: This could be training you have gone through or training you have done for others. If you have experience as a trainer, you would include examples of classes you have taught or skills you have trained others on. If you have gone through any training that is notable, put that information in this section. If you received a certificate upon completion of that training, include a copy. It could be computer training, sales training, speaker training, Dale Carnegie training, any special courses you took outside of the normal college classes, and the list goes on and on. This also includes any on-the-job training you received with your current employer.

Performance Reviews: Share your most recent performance reviews from your current job if you are working while going to school. If you worked during the summer, ask your past employer to provide a review of how well you did and what set you apart from the other employees. Most employers are more than happy to do this if you just ask.

The performance review will give examples of where you have shined in your past position. It will also give examples of where you can improve. Many people think that by sharing areas where they need to improve they could be hurting themselves, but I believe the opposite is true—by showing a performance review where you needed to work on a particular area, you are able to share the steps you took to improve and how that made you a better employee. When people are interviewing you, they want to know how you take direction. They want to know whether you take suggestions well and then how you implement them. It's also a good indicator of how you will do in a future position.

Sales Results: If you are ever in a sales position or a position that used numbers to display achievement, this is your opportunity to let the numbers speak for you. Print out both past and current figures; this will give a good history of your performance over time. When asked by an interviewer to give an example of your past performance, by having solid numbers down on paper, you're setting yourself up for success. It's easy to give an answer, but without proof the interviewer is left to question if your figures are truly factual. Don't leave any room for doubt. Do your best to have numbers that are on company reports; this way the interviewer is not wondering whether you created them. You can also include graphs depicting your sales numbers, but don't get carried away. Keep it simple and to the point.

Coaching Forms: Many companies now give out coaching forms to their employees. These are forms given out by your manager or anyone that may be observing your work. They provide feedback as to how you are doing and areas to work on. Coaching forms are a much simpler form than a business review. They are usually based on one day's worth of watching you work. Coaching forms highlight your strengths as well as areas for improvement. By including these forms, you are sharing how you have responded to areas where you have needed growth. Being willing to share this data will show how you have addressed shortfalls and how you have improved, thus giving potential employers a sense of how well you will fit into their company. We're not perfect. Let me say that again, *we're not perfect.* And that means *you.* So don't look at a coaching form as a negative.

Everyone needs coaching in one way or another; take this opportunity to use it to show how you take direction and how you respond to direction.

Goals or Goal Planning: Companies are looking for people who can achieve and beat the goals set for them. They also like to see people take the initiative to set their own goals. In this section you would include examples of how you planned out how you were going to achieve the goals the company had set for you or goals that you set for yourself. Did you have a specific thought process when determining how you would achieve the goals?

An example may be a sheet of paper with your goal listed at the top of the page. Below this you list out (bulleted) all the steps you did to achieve the goal. At the end of the example you would include how you ended up in achieving the goal.

This way you are able to walk a person through your thought process of achieving the goal and then show him the outcome. This shows your ability to think through an objective, determine the best possible ways to achieve a goal, and then implement them for success. It helps the person you are meeting with to understand how you strategize and map out how you are going to not just achieve a goal but exceed it.

Recruiting: Do you have experience in recruiting? Maybe you have been responsible for hiring someone or maybe you helped in the process. If you ever have direct responsibility for hiring for a specific position you could include questions you asked the candidates along with an outline of what you were looking for when interviewing a candidate.

Maybe you were not ultimately responsible for the hiring of a position but you sat in on the interviews to gain experience for future roles within a company. In this case maybe you were given some direction to ask questions and give feedback on what you thought of the candidates. This is also great experience and should be shared. Each thing you do provides valuable experience that helps set you apart from others.

Partnering: This is a great place to show off your interpersonal skills. Do you have examples of when you partnered with a customer to help reach a goal? Were you able to help the customer achieve his or her goals while at the same time achieving yours? What steps did you take to accomplish this?

Notable Accomplishments: Are there certain accomplishments that you are really proud of that don't fit into another area? Like I said earlier, be flexible in creating your sections, and if there is something that is truly important and would benefit you greatly by being shared but it does not fit into any other section, create a section for it.

Again, this is only the tip of the iceberg of the different types of sections you may have. Depending on your background and the position for which you are applying, you may have completely different sections. Think of what would be important for the specific position and create your sections around that. If you are going after a greater raise, create your sections around the areas where you have had the greatest impact for the company. Lastly, have fun!

Enjoy the process of putting this together and the opportunity to share your success.

6

Situational Planning:
Preparing Your Answers to Their Questions

"There comes a time in a man's life when to get where he has to go—if there are not doors or windows—he walks through a wall."
-Bernard Malamud

If you are serious about getting hired you need to let it show. As you move along in your career you also need to show your passion when it comes to getting a larger raise or being selected for a promotion. As the quote states, sometimes you must go through a wall. Don't stop now! Keep reading and know that you are going to succeed. Take the time to prepare and it will pay off in the end.

In this section are interview scenarios you may experience. You will be given examples of how to answer questions using the Success Portfolio you're creating. You will also learn how to use your portfolio in a situation when you are going for future promotion or during a review for a raise. I have included many examples that you would use for future interviews but again, look them over because you may see how a past experience you have had will work for this example.

During an interview, meeting for a possible promotion, or review, you will need to be able to give examples of your past experience. That's why knowing how to use your Success Portfolio is so important. The key is to use your portfolio as *support*, not the end all be all. You should first be able to share your example and then use your portfolio to back up your example and bring validity.

Never bring out your portfolio at the beginning of the interview; wait until you begin to answer questions.

Generally, in the beginning of an interview you will be asked to tell a little about yourself, why you want the job, why you are looking to make a change, etc. You may even be asked if you have an extra copy of your resume incase there is someone there that did not get a copy. Make sure you bring a few extra copies of your resume that are not in your Success Portfolio. This way you can give them the resume without having to bring out your portfolio just yet.

You want to wait until you are asked the more detailed questions where they are looking for specific examples. Then, *before* you show them your portfolio, you want to first answer the question using the method I will explain below and *then* bring out your Success Portfolio. At that time you would provide each person you are meeting with a copy of your portfolio. Ask them to turn to a specific section and then let them know which page they need to turn to within that section. Once there, walk them through the example in a concise manner. Once you have given them your Success Portfolio, don't ask for it back; it's theirs to keep. Let them keep it, because the goal is to have them reference it throughout the interview. It's a great way to put a solid exclamation point on your response to a question.

Paint a picture with words to make your experience come alive.

It is helpful during the interview process to use words to paint a picture. This keeps the interviewer involved. You need to help them see things through your eyes. To do this, you need to put your answers to their questions in the form of a story. Let me share an easy way to remember how to respond to a question, using a simple acronym: *STAR*. Start by sharing the *S*ituation. Provide background of the situation so they understand the starting point. Then move into the *T*ask that needed to be done to move things along. What did you do to prepare for this particular situation? Next share the *A*ction you took to get things done, to get the business, and to achieve the goal, and close with the *R*esult. By putting your answers in this format, you are helping the person get the whole picture of what happened in your example. This STAR method is used by many top companies when interviewing. If you are going for a review or promotion, you should also use this method. By sharing your example in this format, you show that you were able to think through the process and put action to your plan. By closing with the results and showing them an example in your binder, you bring everything home and wrap it up in a powerful way. You will see the STAR method used in this chapter when answering example questions.

When preparing to answer a question, don't be afraid to take your time. It's perfectly okay not to jump right in and blurt out an answer. In fact, it's better to take a breath, count to three, and then answer the question. Use this time to decide which example you want to share and which one would best get across your experience. You may have a couple of examples you could use, so you want to think for just a few seconds which would provide the best opportunity to highlight your Success Portfolio. You don't want to take a long time, but just enough for you to think through the question and catch your breath. There have been times where I have taken as long as ten seconds to answer a question, and in those situations I have said, "That's a great question, and I have a few examples I could share. May I take just a moment to determine which would best answer your question?" This buys you a little more time, but you only want to do this once or twice in an interview, and you also want to make sure you really do have multiple answers to this question in case they ask you to share more examples.

Most likely, you will not share all your examples in your port-folio during an interview. If there are some examples you feel should be shared and would be beneficial for the interviewer to know, ask them at the end of the interview if it would be okay to share something with them. Remember, this may be your only chance to let them know about you, so take advantage of the time. Usually this is done at the end of the interview when they ask you if you have any questions for them. At this time you can simply say, "I do have some questions, but first I have a few examples we did not cover that I feel would be very important for you to know. Would you mind if I took just a few minutes to go over them?" You will find that they will almost always tell you to go right ahead. Remember, if you want this job, promotion, or raise, you need to take charge and take control of your future. Keep your examples brief and get to the point; remember that you will be leaving your binder with them, so they will be able to go back and take a closer look. You just want to make sure you take advantage of this opportunity to share areas that would be of particular interest to the position for which you are applying.

A word to the wise: many times you will be asked to share one example of your greatest strength and/or your greatest weakness. You have done your homework and are ready to answer any of these questions, and then the person interviewing you says, "What is your next greatest weakness?" You were ready to answer the question with one example, but not with a second. Sometimes this is done to see just how prepared you are. Most people come ready to give one example to a question asked, but they are not ready to give another example. Keep in the back of your mind another example you can use just in case you are asked to provide an additional one. Don't let this follow-up question throw you.

This chapter will not even come close to touching all the questions you may be asked. That's why I want to share a book that I believe will help you: *Knock 'em Dead: Great Answers to over 200 Tough Interview Questions*. It gives you a solid foundation of questions that may be asked of you and helps you to understand what the interviewer is really looking for by asking you certain questions. Also, take full advantage of your schools career department. They will usually have additional resources that provide questions you may be asked.

Situational Questions

Question: "*Tell me about a time when you had to work with a team and there was conflict.*" Think about a time when you have worked on a paper with multiple people, participated in a class project with a team, been on a sports team and the list goes on. You may have also worked full- or part-time while in school and could use a teaming example from that experience.

Answer: "During a recent project for a business class, I was given the opportunity to be the leader. It was my job to make sure everything ran smoothly and was finished on time. We were working in a team of four, and each person was given a specific task to do. One of the team members was not pulling his weight, and it began to put stress on the whole team. As leader, I took it upon myself to talk to this person and share my feelings and how his performance was affecting the team and the project. By going to him wanting to help rather than put him down, I was able to convey that I was truly interested in him and what may be going on. In talking to this person I found out he was under a lot of stress with other projects and some issues at home. By taking the time to understand instead of jumping to conclusions, I was able to better understand this person's situation and also share with him the importance of getting this project done correctly and on time. Through this process I was able to help him prioritize some of the things he had on his plate and free up more time for this project. I'm happy to say that we finished on time and we got an A on the project.

"If you would turn in the portfolio to the section labeled Projects, you will see the example I just shared. This a brief outline of the project, how we broke the work out and the outcome. Through this example I learned that teaming will have its challenges, but by taking the time to understand and not jump to conclusions, you're better able to make the right decisions and build a stronger team. I also learned the importance of leading by example. By this I mean not to jump to conclusions but to go to the person and talk. Through talking and especially listening I was able to move our project along with everyone involved."

Question: "Tell me about yourself." (Note: In this question you don't want to ramble on for ten minutes, but you also want to portray a favorable image of yourself and one that will set you apart. You can even ask a follow up question before answering this question, which I have done on many occasions. It could go something like, "I would be happy to tell you about me, would you like to hear a little about my personal history and then share some of my working experience?" This will clarify for you exactly where to go without sharing too much information. You want to be careful as to not go into detail about family, children, etc. Keep it focused on you and your history.)

Answer: "I was born and raised in Richmond, Virginia. I attended college at Campbell University and later went back to school while working full time to get my MBA. I enjoy traveling, running, hiking, and just being in the great outdoors. I especially like trying to get a picture of the perfect sunset. I also like to get a good book and read when I have the chance. I have been working hard while in school to get good grades while working part time. I have learned how to organize and prioritize my time because of this. I have won many awards and have had the opportunity to mentor others. At the same time I have had some great mentors that have helped me achieve my success along the way. One of the many things I have learned is to listen and learn from others. My time at Campbell University along with my past experience both at school and back at home have prepared me for success. I am excited to be here today and look forward to sharing more of my experiences and accomplishments throughout the interview."

Question: "What sets you apart from any other candidates applying for this position?" Or they may ask "What makes you the best candidate for this position?"

Answer: "I know that I'm the best candidate for this position for several of the reasons I stated earlier, such as my solid experience within this area, my success in past positions, and the fact that I am a team player who is ready to do what's needed to get the job done. I am a self-starter, passionate, and ready to bring my skills (list out a few key skills that really make you stand out) to this position and to this company. I also would like to share a few other reasons that are in my porfolio that we did not cover earlier if that's okay. If you turn to the third tab, titled "Achievements," you'll see I'm certified in making widgets and that I was awarded the best widget-maker in Widget County. I feel that these examples really set me apart from all others and make me the best person for this position.

"Based on this information, I know that I am the best person for this position, and I want this position. Is there any reason based on what I have shared with you that you don't agree I am the best person for this position?"

Note: This may be uncomfortable for you to ask, but this will set you apart in a very good way because most other candidates won't ask this question. At this time they could answer, "No, there is no rea-son."

Then you should come back with "When would you like me to start?"

If they answer by saying, "Well, we can't answer that because we have not completed our interview process and have a few others after you." If this is the case, you could ask, "Based on whom you have interviewed, do you believe I am the top candidate so far?" If they say no, ask why not and whether there is a specific area you lack that they are looking for. You want to make sure you understand any questions they may have concerning any area they feel you may be lacking.

One thing to keep in mind is this: know when to take a step back and stop pushing. You want to be aggressive enough to show them your interest, but not so much so that you turn them off. You also want them to know you believe in yourself, but you don't want to go over the line.

Question: "What have you done to prepare for this inter-view?" (Note: They are looking to see if you did anything outside of the norm like searching the internet. Did you get creative and really go above and beyond or just play it safe?"

Answer: "I did the typical research, I went on the internet and found out some interesting information on your company such as (you fill in the blank on anything that caught your eye, maybe it was their mission statement or a list of goals they have.) I also did some things that are probably not typical. I searched many of the top newspapers both local and national to see if there were any recent articles on your company. I also researched who some of your customers are and spoke with one of them, XZY Corporation. I told them that I was going to be interviewing for a position with this company and I wanted to get their feedback on how they view this company. I spoke with Mr. Tim Johnson in purchasing and he was able to provide some great information.

If you will turn to the tab titled "Research" you will see the questions I asked Mr. Johnson and his response to these questions. (*Note*: you could also include one or two articles you may have found from a newspaper behind the page containing the questions you asked the customer.) He spoke very favorably of your company and gave some great feedback. As you can see from the first question, he definitely thinks this would be a great company for me to work for and help you in achieving the company's goals for success.

After all my research I feel more strongly than ever before that I want to be on your team and help XYZ Company achieve it's goals for success.

Question: "Why should I hire you?" (Note: they are looking to see if you can summarize your skills and abilities and if you believe in yourself. Can you communicate what makes you stand out from all the other candidates?)

Answer: "Because I am the best person for this position. Based on my experience, skills and abilities I know I have what it takes to go above and beyond the expectations of this position. I believe that the supporting documentation I have provided in my Success Portfolio supports this fact. I want this job and I know I will make a great addition to your team. When can I start?" Always end your answer to this question with "I want this job and I know I will make a great addition to your team. When can I start?" Then don't say a word.

You would not believe the number of people who never ask for the job. They never tell the person interviewing them they want this position. You have just successfully done both. Now let them answer. In most all cases they will say that they have other candidates they must interview and that they can't give you a response right now. If that's the case you should ask one more question. "I can certainly appreciate that. I just want you to know that I want this position and that I am ready to start. If you don't mind me asking, based on everything we have talked about today is there any reason you would not hire me if you did not have other candidates to interview?" Wow, you have just blown their socks off by asking such a great question. They may come back and say, no there no other reason but they may come back and tell you of a specific area that you are lacking in that they were looking for. If that is the case and you have experience in that area but you never were able to share that now is the time to present that information. Either way, you are building a stronger case for why you are the right person for the position.

Question: How has your education prepared you for your career?

Answer: My education has focused me not only on the learning and fundamentals, but also on practical application of the information I learned. For example, I played a lead role in a class project were we gathered and analyzed data from a particular industry. Let me tell you more about the results. If you turn to the tab projects you will see this exact example." Now walk them thru the example briefly.

Question: Have you had a conflict with a boss or professor? How was it resolved? (Note: you want to show how you seek first to understand and that you don't just jump to conclusions.)

Answer: "Yes, I have had conflicts in the past. Never major ones, but there have been disagreements that needed to be resolved. I have found that when conflicts need to be resolved it always helps to seek first to understand before jumping to conclusions. It helps when you fully understand the other person's perspective. I take time to listen to their point of view, and then seek to work out a solution that works for both of us. For example…" Now give a specific time when such an example took place. Keep it brief but show how by working together you were able to resolve the conflict and move forward to a successful outcome. Generally, you would not have a tab titled "Conflicts" because it may look like you cause a lot of conflicts. This would be a question you would answer without using your portfolio in most cases.

Question: **"What kind of salary are you looking for?"** (Note: be very careful how you answer this question. In fact you don't want to throw out a figure if at all possible. Just in case you are pushed to throw out a figure do your research and go to www.Salary.com. Search for the type of job you're interviewing for or something close to it to get an idea of the average this type of position pays. Once you have this information you are ready to answer if pushed for a figure. If at all possible you want to see if the person will give you a salary range they have for this position but many times they will not provide this. Also, you would rarely be asked this question on a first interview.)

Answer: Naturally, I want to make as much as my background, experience and skills would allow. I truly believe I am the right candidate for this job, and after sharing everything in my Success Portfolio, I believe I have been able to support this. Because of this I am sure you will make me a fair offer. Is there a range for this position or did you have a figure in mind? (After asking this, don't say a word. Wait for their response.)

You could also respond by saying: "I would expect a salary appropriate to my experience, skills and ability to do the job successfully. What range do you have in mind?"

At this point they will typically provide a salary range, but not always. If they do give you a range of $36,000 - $41,000 as an example you would want to come back with a response like, "We definitely have something to talk about. I was looking for a minimum of

$40,000 with the ideal being $44,000. Is there any room for negation or flexibility?"

If they don't want to provide a range and really push for you to provide a figure that's when you provide an answer based on what you found out on www.Salary.com You would answer by saying "I did some research on the internet looking at positions like this one and similar and what I found was they typically were in the range of $37,000 to $43,000. Does that seem correct for this position and the range you are looking at providing?" They then may come back with "Yes, that range is a little high but close. Is there a certain amount in that range you were looking to receive?" You would then defer to the example I shared above on using the range and pick a figure at the high end of the range. "I was looking for a minimum of $42,000 with the ideal being $45,000. Is there any room for negation or flexibility?"

Question: If I were to ask your boss or professor to describe you, what would they say? (Note: before ever getting to the interview you should have asked a previous boss to write a reference letter for you. Also, ask a couple of teachers to write a reference letter for you describing what they feel sets you apart and makes you special. Then when you are asked this question you already have the answer ready for them to read!)

Answer: "I believe they would say I'm a hard worker that is focused and passionate about what I do. I am an eager and energetic person that is results oriented. I believe they would also say I have been one of the best people he or she has worked with. In fact, if you turn to the "References" tab in the portfolio you will see these exact words in a letter of recommendation my previous boss and professor wrote." Then briefly walk them through the letter and close by saying, "As you can see they think very highly of me and my abilities. Are the qualities they shared in the letter the type of qualities you are looking for in the person that will fill this position?" After the person says "yes" you can close this question with, "Well, I'm ready to start tomorrow if you are." This is a great way to show how much you want the position and also show that you have the qualities they are looking for. They will come back and say that they have other applicants they must meet with but hey, you sure have raised that bar so high it's going to be almost impossible for anyone else to come close.

Question: "Are you willing to relocate? How about in the future?" (Note: be honest in your question. Hopefully you know where the position you are interviewing for is located and if it's not where you currently live and you don't want to move you should not be interviewing for it in the first place.)

Answer: "Absolutely. I understand that this position would be located in Somewhere Town, USA and I'm excited about learning a new area and starting my career with you there." "As far as the future goes and if I would be willing to relocate, a lot would depend on the position. If given the opportunity to expand my role with XYZ Company and it was a good fit for both the company and myself, I don't see any reason why I would not be willing to relocate." A lot can change in a few years. Maybe you get married and start to have a family and you decide you don't want to move. Remember in your response, you said if it was a good fit for you and the company. It may not be a good fit for you then and that would be fine but you don't need to go into all that reasoning during this interview.

Question: "Tell me about a time when you failed to meet a goal or objective." (Note: They are looking to see how you handle rejection in not meeting a goal. Do you give up or can you persevere? You have a great opportunity to turn this question into a success if properly done, like below. The example below is one that would be used after working for some time but you can see how you could insert your own example into the below example and make it work.)

Answer: "Well, one time I had situation where I had been trying to work with a customer for quite some time. This customer did approximately half a million dollars in business with our largest competitor. My goal was to earn his business, but it proved to be harder than what I had expected. It was a quite large company with many levels of decision makers. It ultimately funneled down to the director of purchasing who had the final decision. I had been working on this for over six months and had established a good relationship with the director of purchasing. It looked like we were going to get the business when an issue with one of our products came up. When this happened it was like putting the brakes on everything we had worked on up to now. The company was concerned with our products and if they would hold up to its use and decided not to move their business. Needless to say I was quite disappointed but I did not give up. While our company was looking into the issue I stayed in constant contact with this customer, giving updates on what was happening. I asked that he continue to hang in there and allow me the opportunity to show him that moving the business over to our company would be the right decision. It took an additional three months for everything to get corrected. Because of my persistence and excellent communication with this potential customer throughout the situation, I ultimately achieved my goal of earning the business.

"Later the customer told me that they really appreciated how I worked with them while we were correcting the issue. They felt confident that if anything in the future was to ever happen that we would take care of them. What could have been a disaster turned out to be an opportunity to show this customer the exceptional customer service we provide, which in turn helped earn their trust and the business.

Things are going to happen in every business, it's how you react to them that makes the difference. I stayed focused on the customer, kept him informed of what was going on, and made sure I provided the best possible service. I talked with all those involved in the process but was able to establish the ultimate decision maker and build a solid working relationship that ultimately got us the business.

"If you will turn to the "Success Stories" section in the portfolio you will see the result of the example I just shared with you. Let me share with you what you are looking at. The page you are looking as provides a brief overview of the potential business they had. The graph shows the growth we have experienced over the past year. They have grown by 13% with even more potential in the future."

Note: This is a great time to ask a follow-up question once you are done answering the question and walking them through the example in your binder. "How does your company respond to existing and potential customers when issues arise?" If you don't have an example to share where you successfully turned things around, be upfront and honest. After you tell them the results, share why you feel you were not successful and what you would do differently. What did you learn from not reaching this goal and or objective? This shows that when setbacks happen (and believe me they will), you look for ways to learn from them.

Question: "What have you done to improve yourself?"

Answer: "I like to stay at the top of what's going on in the industry, so I strive to look for ways to improve my knowledge. One of the things I'm most proud of is receiving my MBA. I went through an Executive MBA program, which had me going to class at night while working during the day. (This could also be additional courses in a specific career field.) I have taken courses in selling both through my company and on my own. I receive the trade publications pertaining to this industry to help me stay on top of the latest developments. I just recently took a leadership course that helped me have a better understanding of working with others and the difference between being a manager and being a leader. I also like to get out a couple times a week and run. I like to work on improving both my career side as well as my health.

"If you turn to the "Continuing Education" section of the portfolio, you will see a copy of my MBA transcript along with certificates from the sales courses I have taken."

Note: You may want to ask a question of them to get their buy in of what you have done and to see if there are other areas they are looking for. "How does my work to improve myself compare to what you look for in a candidate? Are there any other areas you would like to see that I did not share with you?"

Additional Questions

The following is a list of questions that you could be asked in an interview. Take some time to think about each of them. Look for a way to answer them so you can incorporate your answer into an example in your Success Portfolio. Then write down your potential answers and keep them in your filing system to review before your next interview.

- What is your greatest weakness? What is your greatest strength?
- What did you do to prepare for this interview?
- Why did you choose to attend this school? (Note: You want to show a lot of thought went into your decision.

Maybe it was due to cost and that is fine to say but also include other reasons like great programs they offer etc...)

- What motivates you?
- Tell me about a time you had to take charge to get something done?
- Tell me about a time you had a disagreement with your manager or professor?
- Why did you choose this career to enter into?
- What interests you about this job?
- Are you a team player?
- Tell me about a time you were given some criticism? How did you take it?
- What do you want to do in three to five years?
- Tell me about a time when you exceeded the company's goals or your own goals?
- Tell me about a time when you exceeded a teacher's goal for a project?
- How do you define success? How do you define failure?
- What is your favorite class and why?
- Who were your favorite professors and why?

7

How To's:

How to End the Interview

When the interview is near completion, you generally will be asked if you have any questions for your interviewers. At this time you want to ask any questions you may have. Have a list of questions prior to coming to the interview. This shows them that you are organized and have really thought things out. Typically three to five questions is a good number to ask. Also, if this is your first interview, you don't want to bring up money or detailed information on benefits, bonuses, etc. This is information that is discussed at later interviews. If they don't bring this topic up, stay away from it. By asking this on the first interview it shows that you are more interested in the money than the position or the company.

Here are some questions to choose from and to get you thinking of others:

- What are the top two challenges facing the person coming into this position?
- What's most important to you when making a decision on who would be the best person for this position?

- What are the opportunities for growth / advancement for this position?

- What do you consider to be the key competencies for this position?

- What would be the top one or two expectations of me coming into this position?

- What is it about XYZ Company that made you want to be a part of the company?

- What do you consider to be the key critical success factors for this position?

- What are the top one or two things you are constantly thinking about in your department?

- Why should I want to work for XYZ Company?

- What are the greatest challenges and the greatest opportunities facing the person in this position?

You now want to close for the position. Let them know that they can keep the portfolio for their records and review. And now you want to ask for the position by saying something like, "Based on all the information I have shared with you including the examples I have shown you, I know that I am the best candidate for this position and I want you to know that I want this position. Based on everything I have gone over, is there anything keeping you from offering me this position right now?" Once you ask this, *don't say another word.* Let them answer before you speak again. There may be a few moments of awkward silence, but that's okay; give them time to answer. You may be thinking that you could never be so direct and ask such a question. Well, if you don't want the position, then don't ask the question. Remember, most people that never get what they want never asked for it.

"If you don't ask then you won't get. But if you will simply ask for what you want, then you will be amazed at what you get."
-James Malinchak

The person or people interviewing you want to know if you truly want the position. If there is something keeping them from offering you the position, you want to know what it is before you leave. If they tell you that there is something missing, follow up by asking them what it is. It may be one key area they are looking for that you have experience in but that never came up during the interview.

They may come back and tell you that they are not ready to make a decision at this time because they have others to interview or a number of other reasons. You need to respect their answer and reiterate that you are the best person for the position. At this point the next thing to ask is, "Where do we go from here? What is the next step and when could I expect to hear back from you?" If they give you a time, such as within a week, you could ask, "Would it be okay to follow up with you next Friday if I have not heard back from you by then?" By setting a specific date, it shows follow through and your commitment. It also gives you another opportunity to talk with them and see if they have any additional questions.

If the person you are interviewing with is not the person that is going to be making the final decision, you can simply ask the following: "Is there anything keeping you from supporting me and recommending me for this position to the person in charge of hiring?" They may not be making the final decision, but they would not be interviewing you if they did not have some say in it. If you can get their buy in, you are one step closer to getting the job.

Make sure you thank them for their time and the opportunity to interview and tell them that you are looking forward to hearing from them. As soon as you can, within twenty-four hours, write a thank-you note to each person with whom you interviewed. When writing the thank you, make sure you spell the person's name correctly and have his or her correct title in the address line. A good thank-you note is worth its weight in gold. It's one more opportunity to get your name in front of them, and it shows your overall commitment to detail. The thank-you note does not need to be long; just a couple of paragraphs are all you need. Start off by thanking them for their time and let them know how nice it was getting to know them. You then want to bring out just one or two key points that were important to them and restate how your experience has prepared you to make an immediate impact to this area or areas. Close by stating your desire for the position and how you are the best person for the position. Include your address, phone number, and e-mail address to make sure they have all the ways to contact you.

How to Prepare for a Second Interview

Congratulations! You made it past the first interview and have been asked to come back for a second interview with the same person or other people within the company. What do you do now? Relax; because you took the time to prepare for the first interview, you are ready. In this next round you may meet with a group of people together or individually. They may set up the interview so that you meet with many different people from many areas of the company. You may be asked to have a seat in a board room where you will stay during the interviews and the other people will come in to meet with you, or you may go around to the different offices of the people that are going to interview you. There are quite a number of examples of how this can work. Even though you are meeting with more people, your plan is still the same in using your Success Portfolio. If possible, find out how many people you will be interviewing with and also their names and titles. This will help you in preparing for the interview and it also lets you know how many Success Portfolios you need to make and bring with you. You want to have one for each person interviewing you.

It's a good rule of thumb to make one copy of your Success Portfolio for each person that you will be doing a sit down interview with. It's also good to bring one or two extra copies just in case someone else joins in. Remember to always keep one copy for yourself so you will have one to refer to during the interview. If you come up short because they added someone for you to meet with at the last minute, just share your copy with them and ask if they would like for you to forward a copy once you return home.

If you find yourself having a sit-down interview with multiple people, you will want to make a set of questions that you want to ask each person ahead of time. What I have done before is put the person's name I will be meeting with at the top of the page for you to refer to during the interview. Next, list out the questions you would like to ask this person at the end of the interview when they will typically ask you, "Do you have any questions for me?" Remember to leave room between each question for you to write down their answer. The best scenario is to have these questions typed out. Then when you are done with one interview, you file that sheet of paper away and you bring out the next set of questions that you have already put together for the next person you will be meeting with.

I know it goes without saying, but be nice to everyone you meet. If you are going to the company headquarters, get to know the receptionist at the front desk. Be polite to everyone, because never again will you get the chance to make a good first impression, and you never know if that person may provide feedback on how you treated him or her.

How to Accomplish a Pay Increase

If you are using the Success Portfolio to get a greater pay increase in your current position, take the lead when meeting with your manager, director, or whomever you report. Ask for some time to meet, letting them know you have some valuable information you would like to share. You will not be sitting down answering the previous interview questions as if you were interviewing for a job. You will, however, be sitting down with them and explaining why you deserve an increase that is more fitting to your contributions and achievements while in your current role.

Also, if you were given an increase that you don't feel was enough, you need to take it upon yourself and ask for the opportunity to share some information with your manager.

At this time you want to let your manager know that you appreciate the increase you received but that you don't agree with the amount. Share that you were expecting a larger increase based on the work you had done. You need to be able to express what you have done, achieved, and/or created while in the position. Give your portfolio to your manager and briefly share its contents, pointing out any highlights that you feel support your request the best. Explain that you are going to leave this with him or her to review and based on the information provided, you were looking to receive an increase of X%.

Thank your manager for his time and say that you look forward to hearing back.

Personal example: Let me share with you an example of when I did this very thing. When I was working for a large transportation company early on in my career, I experienced just such a scenario. I had been working my heart out for the past year and had taken on many leadership roles. I felt sure that I would be receiving a 12 to15% increase at my upcoming performance review. Instead of having a sit-down performance review, my manager met with me very informally and told me he was excited to be giving me a 6% increase. Although 6% was not bad, it sure was not what I had imagined. My mind began to race with all the things I had done over the past year. Why did he not see the value I brought to the table? How could he give me such a small raise? Granted, most people would be very happy with a 6% increase, but you and I are not most people!

Well, because I had been keeping my Success Portfolio updated and had come prepared just in case, I was ready to take action. I told him that while I appreciated the increase, it was below the percent increase that I was expecting. He then asked me what I was expecting, so I told him I was expecting a 16% increase. I could tell he was thinking, "Yeah, right, in your dreams!" I went on to tell him that this may seem large in relation to the amount that he originally gave me but that I strongly felt that after he reviewed my Success Portfolio that he would see the reasoning for my request. I pointed out a few areas of real importance, which included a few large projects that I had spearheaded over the past year. I then told him that I would leave the Success Portfolio with him to look over and that I felt that after looking it over he would agree that I deserved a 16% increase.

The following day my manager called me into his office and told me he had not realized all that I had done over the past year. He thanked me for sharing the information and went on to tell me that I would be receiving a 16% increase! This would never have happened if I had just told him that I thought I deserved a larger increase without providing the supporting documentation. Now, I understand that you will not always be able to get such a large increase, but if you never ask, you can be certain that you will never receive anything larger than what you were given. Maybe you won't get the full amount you had requested, but you have a great shot of having them increase it above the original amount. One thing is for sure: if you don't ask, you most certainly won't get it. If you don't believe in yourself and your worth, don't expect others to.

Many departments are given an amount for raises and must split that budget between all in the department. This does not give a lot of room for large increases, but you never know what can happen. In my case, the manager went back to his director and shared my portfolio with him. They were able to find additional money to provide the additional increase. I have not always gotten such large increases in my career. I have gone from getting a 3% increase to a 5% increase in another example. In this case the company had not met the projected goals it had set and did not make the money it had expected. Because of this, all increases were small and an additional 2% increase was quite generous.

In many cases, your manager may have to get approval from someone above him or her, and without documentation as to why you deserve such an increase, they would not be able to go to bat for you and get the increase. Don't rely on your manager knowing all that you do. They are busy and in most cases have multiple people reporting to them. They may have documentation on some of your accomplishments, but it's up to you to keep complete records.

If you have done the work and have performed your job above and beyond expectations, you need to make sure your manager knows just what you have done. They will remember the last thing you did and maybe a few others but likely will have forgotten many of the other accomplishments. It's up to you to make them aware of all you have done and the value you bring to the company!

Note: Ask to meet with the person you report to prior to yearly raises being given out. This will give him or her time to make adjustments prior to informing everyone of their increase. It's easier for them to make adjustments up front instead of waiting till after everyone has been given a raise.

> *"All our dreams can come true—*
> *if we have the courage to pursue them."*
> **-Walt Disney**

I know that you may be saying to yourself, "I can never tell a future boss I don't agree with the increase given to me." You may be thinking, "What if he gets mad?" Or, "What if she lowers my increase?" Or, "What if he fires me?" Let me ask you a question: What if your manager actually increased your raise? What if she saw the value you brought to the company and not only increased your raise but looked to you for a promotion? You will only find this out by asking. Managers what to know that their employees believe in themselves and that they are willing to stand up for what they believe in. This shows that you will also do that for the company. It's okay to be nervous, but don't let that keep you from standing up for what you deserve. If you don't ask, you will never know if you could have gotten a larger raise, and that should be enough to make you take a stand. If you put your Success Portfolio together correctly, you will be prepared and will have all the backing to support your request. So get out there and show them what your worth!

"Don't wait for your ship to come; swim out to it."
-Anonymous

"If opportunity doesn't knock, build a door."
-Milton Berle

8

Bringing It All Together:

How to Assemble Your Success Portfolio

"The greatest amount of wasted time is the time not getting started."
- Dawson Trotman

Check out a sample picture of a Success Portfolio

at the end of this chapter.

You are almost there. You are just about ready to begin the process of creating your own Success Portfolio. Believe me when I say the work will be worth it. Nothing worthwhile in life ever comes easy; if it did, everyone would do it. I am proud of you for reading this far; that is the first step. You have already given your time to go this far, so don't stop now. The worst thing you can do is put this down and say, "I will start on it tomorrow or the next day or the next day." When you start procrastinating, you are already halfway down the road of defeat. Start gathering your information today. Begin writing down the titles of your sections today. Call a friend and tell him or her about this and work on your Success Portfolios together. Just make sure you start working on it today. Roll up your sleeves and get ready to help yourself become a success, and don't procrastinate, begin today! The sooner you begin the closer you are to achieving

your dreams and goals.

"You don't have to see the whole staircase, just take the first step."
- **Martin Luther King Jr.**

"Procrastination is the fear of success. People procrastinate because they are afraid of the success that they know will result if they move ahead now. Because success is heavy, carries a responsibility with it, it is much easier to procrastinate and live on the "someday I'll philosophy."
- **Denis Waitley**

Once you have gathered your information and decided on the

section titles of your portfolio, you are ready to put it all together. You

have a few options in how you assemble your binder. When I began

creating my first binder I used a three-ring binder. It is the most cost

effective and easy to put together. This may be the best solution for

you now, especially since you will be providing a copy to everyone

you are meeting with.

"Spending money on improving yourself is not an expense, it's an investment in your future."
-**Stephen Jennings**

As you move along in your career I would suggest moving

towards using a spiral or comb binding that provides a more profes-

sional look. The spiral binding is very professional, allows for the

pages to turn easily, and looks sharp. If you are serious about standing out and making a great impression, I would suggest investing a few extra dollars and using the spiral binding. The comb binding is also a good choice but it can be hard to turn the pages as your Success Portfolio increases in size as your experience increases.

If you go with a three ring binder, you should use a dark blue or black binder that has a clear cover where you would slide your cover sheet with your name and contact information. If you go with a spiral binding, I would suggest using a clear cover for the front and a dark blue or black cover for the back. The clear front cover allows for your title page with your name and contact information to stand out where everyone can see. The back cover helps protect your information and also gives it the finished look.

If you choose to use a spiral or comb binding, I would then suggest taking all of your work (already in the order you want) to a copy store or retail office store. They will be able to put it together and attach the backing, cover, and coil or comb binding. I have also had them create the tabs for me, which gives it a nice finished look. You can create your own tabs, and I have done that in the past, but I was never able to get them to all be straight and have the neat appearance as the ones the copy store could do. This will add to the cost so be sure to ask for the estimate before you hand everything over. If you do have the store create the tabs, you will need to provide them with the different titles for each tab and the order you want them in.

I take Post-It notes and at the beginning of each new section I put a Post-It note at the top of a blank piece of paper so the note is sticking out above the other papers. This blank piece of paper will be placed at the beginning of each new section. On the note I write the title of that section. This shows them the title to create for the tab and where to place it. The tabs will be on the side of the binder, making it easy to read. Make sure you keep your tab titles short. It will be difficult for them to put multiple words on a small tab. Try to think of the best one word that describes each section. If you must use multiple words, try to keep them short.

Also, a word to the wise: Typically, most places will be able to have this completed within twenty-four hours, if not sooner, but give yourself some extra time just in case something comes up. **I strongly suggest you ask for a proof copy to be made**. They can make one copy for you to come back and look at, making sure everything is in the order you want and turned out the way you were expecting. This is a great idea, especially for your first success portfolio. You don't want to order five portfolios only to find out that something is not right. This may add another day in getting all your binders, but its well worth it to save you from spending money on something that was not correct. You are now ready to create your portfolio!

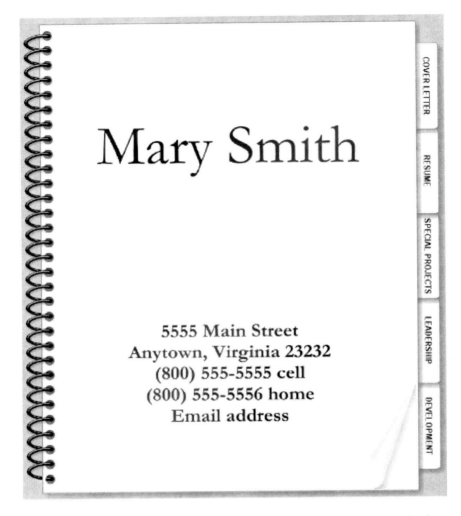

This shows how a Success Portfolio could look using a spiral
binding with a clear front cover.

This shows examples of tabs that could be used and how it could look. This example shows tabs that were done by me and not by an office store. If you were to have the office store create the tabs they would be printed directly on the tabs.

9

Last Minute Tips:
What to Do & Not Do Before, During & After the Interview

- **First and foremost, PRAY!** Give thanks to God for the opportunity you have been given. Turn over any stress and worry you may have and ask for wisdom. Go forward in confidence.

- **Research, research, research the companies you are interviewing with.** You should of course do the typical research by looking at the company Web site, but take it a step further. Look for other ways to gather information on the company, such as talking to its customers. Find out some of the customers of the company you are interviewing with and see if they would answer a few questions. Let them know upfront that you are interviewing with XYZ Corporation and that you would like their perspective on the company. How they currently work with them, what they like about the company, and what things they would change.

This information will help you better determine if you actually do want to work for the company. It will also tell you how customers view the company. By taking the time talk with a customer of the company, you will truly set yourself apart from the other candidates. You will be able to use the information you receive to show your interviewers that you went well beyond what most people do by just looking at the company Web site. It shows your initiative and desire to know more about the company and that you are interviewing the company, just as it is interviewing you. This one thing will make a dynamic impression that will turn heads! Give it a try and see for yourself.

When you give your answer, keep it brief and hit the highlights. Start off by sharing the general information you found on the company Web site or in trade publications, such as company's mission, vision, and what they stand for, what their focus is, and who their customers are. Next tell them you wanted to find out about the company from a customer's point of view. Share which customer you met with and give just a few key points you got from your talk. Then tie everything back to how your research of the company only makes you want to be a part of the company even more.

• **Network!** Talk to everyone you can about opportunities they may know about at companies you are interested in working. Let everyone know they type of position you are looking for and ask if they would keep their eyes and ears open for any opportunities they may hear about and let you know. Talk to your parents friends. Talk to people at your church there at school and back at home. Utilize jobs sites like www.Monster.com, www.ChristianJobs.com, www. CarreerBuilder.com, www.USJobs.gov, www.Jobs.com.

Leave no stone unturned. As you talk with people, show them your Success Portfolio so they can see just how prepared you are. This will give them confidence in referring you to someone else. Remember, when someone referrers you, they are putting their name and reputation on the line. By showing them how prepared you are you give them a reason to feel great about their decision to refer you.

Another option is using a headhunter. Here is the key if going this route. Headhunters only get paid if they are able to place a person in a position. Because of this they will push those individuals they feel are going to get hired first. They want to get paid and for that to happen they must put forward the individuals that have the best chance in matching what a company is looking for. Many headhunters don't work with college students because they are not able to show how they will bring the experience needed to get hired by the companies working with that particular headhunter. So what do you do? You must sell yourself! When talking with a headhunter by phone, tell them you would like to send them a copy of your Success Portfolio. Tell that that you believe that after seeing what you bring to the table they will feel confident in promoting you for a position. Most headhunters only receive a resume from people looking for a job. By getting your Success Portfolio, you will stand out and they will know you are serious about getting hired. Most importantly, the headhunter will have the confidence needed to push you forward past other candidates. They will do this because you offer a higher opportunity of getting hired which means they get paid.

- **Ask for a business card from the person or people you are interviewing with** at the beginning of the interview and give the person or people interviewing you one of yours if you have one. If you wait until the end of the interview, you may forget to get one. This will help in writing your thank-you note because it will give you the person's proper title, address, and correct spelling of their name.

- **Always keep good eye contact**. When answering a question, make sure you look the person or people in the eye. The more you look away, down at the floor, or up at the ceiling, it gives the impression you are not sure or that you are hiding something. Eye contact also shows you are listening and interested. You should also look for eye contact from them. If you see them keeping eye contact with you, you have their attention. If not, finish your story quickly and move on. It may be a sign that you are taking a long time to answer their question and they have lost interest.

- **Dress for the position you are interviewing for**. In other words, dress for success. There is not enough paper or time to go over all the mistakes people make when choosing what to wear to an interview so let me give some general direction. When you are interviewing for a position do some research and see what people in that position are wearing. If it's a corporate position you want to dress the part. Don't show up in jeans and a sport coat or a way to short skirt and a tight top. It's always best to dress more conservative. I know this will be difficult for some people but just how badly do you want the job? Now is not the time to put on your brightest colored clothes to "make a statement". You will be making a statement and you will stand out but not in a good way. Your words, actions and especially your Success Portfolio will make you stand out in a great way!

Guys, shine your shoes and if you don't know how find someone to help you.

Invest in a good dark blue or black suit and a white long sleeve dress shirt. It's also good to wear an undershirt under the dress shirt. This way if you do sweet it won't show thru the dress shirt. If you're wearing a blue suit don't wear white socks. Buy a pair of nice blue dress socks.

Girls, same holds true for you. Invest in a nice pants suit or dress (depending on the type of job you're interviewing for.) No short skirts and halter tops. Leave the 6 inch heals at home and go a little more conservative. Also, now is not the time to show off your creative side by having different designs on your finger nails. Paint them one color.

- **It's a good idea to keep your answers to two or three minutes.** Practice answering questions using your Success Portfolio and time yourself. This will help you focus on answering the questions without using a lot of filler words and information. If the person what's you to go into more detail they will ask. You just don't want to ramble on for 10 minutes, this will turn them off.

- **Listen, listen, listen.** Listen for little things they may say that could trigger you to some of their hot buttons. Don't be thinking about what you want to say next. You may miss something important that they are telling you. Stay focused on them and what they are saying to you. They may mention something that would fit perfectly with an example you have, but if you are thinking ahead and not paying attention, you may miss this golden opportunity.

- **Take notes.** It's always polite to ask at the start of the interview if it they would mind if you take notes. I have yet to meet anyone who says, "Yes, I do mind." Have a legal pad in front of you to take notes on. This will help you write down things the person or people say that are important to them. This way you can refer to it later. Note taking is also a sign that you are paying attention and that you are engaged in what is being said. I have had countless people ask me questions while I was interviewing them, never to write down any of my answers. If it was so important to ask, make sure you write it down.

- **Have a clean copy of your résumé along with enough copies for each person interviewing you.** They may have made notes all over it or made copies for others that are there and they did not come out very clear. If you are meeting with multiple people, there is a good chance that only the person you sent your original résumé and cover letter to will have it. The others may not have a copy and may not have seen your résumé. Yes, your Success Portfolio has a copy of your resume and yes, you are going to give them a copy of your portfolio but you want to save your success portfolio for when you get into the question-and-answer part of the interview. You don't want to loose the "wow" factor.

- **Give a firm handshake.** When you meet the person or people interviewing you, make sure you make good eye contact and have a firm handshake. This is also done when you are leaving the interview.

- **What's your name?** If you are asked what you like to be called, don't say, "Anything, or it doesn't matter." If they ask, "Do you like to go by Stephen or Steve?" don't say,

"Either one." Pick one and stay with it. By saying "Either one," or "It doesn't matter," you can be seen as indecisive. I know it's crazy but it's the little things that can make all the difference. I once had a manager that asked this very question to see if I would say "Either one." He was looking to see if I was indecisive. I was later told that he had passed over other candidates because they did say "Either one." I said, "I go by Stephen." I got the job!

- **Don't fidget during the interview**. Try to stay calm. Don't play with your keys or money in your pocket. In fact, it's best to not put change in your pocket so you are not tempted. Keep your hands on your lap or keep them busy by taking notes.

- **Don't bite on your pen, pencil, or fingernails during the interview**.

- **A few minutes before the interview starts, take a quick trip to the restroom** to look in the mirror and make sure you don't have a huge piece of broccoli stuck in your teeth. Also, use this time to dry off your hands if they are sweaty. Just relax.

• **Smile!** If you're excited about the position and the opportunity to interview for it tell your face and smile. This gives a great first impression.

• **Don't interrupt.** No matter how much you want to jump in and answer a question or tell an example, don't interrupt. Even if you have the perfect response or example that will blow them away, DON'T INTERRUPT! There will be plenty of time to share. Let them finish their thoughts, and then take your time in answering. Remember, God gave us two ears and one month because we should listen twice as much as we talk.

• **Sit up straight in your chair**. If you slouch down in the chair it shows a lack of respect.

• **Arrive fifteen minutes early** to give yourself some time to get your thoughts in order, check yourself out in the mirror (for the hunk of broccoli that may be in your teeth), and just to calm yourself down. In fact, if I was not sure of where I was going I would leave enough time just incase I got lost or if there was traffic. With that in mind plan on arriving to the area for the interview 30 minutes ahead of time. When it gets to be about 15 minutes prior to your interview you should go on in and again check yourself out in the mirror for that broccoli.

• **Make sure you have a phone number for the person you are interviewing with** just in case you run into traffic, have a flat tire, or something unexpected comes up that keeps you from making it on time. If nothing else, have the phone number of the place where you are meeting. You can call and have them relay a message.

• **Enjoy!** You have worked hard in getting ready, and now it's your time to shine.

"A dream becomes reality one opportunity at a time.
And if you work like it depends on you and pray like it depends on God,
there is no telling what God can do in you and through you."
Mark Batterson, In a Pit with a Lion on a Snowy Day

LaVergne, TN USA
08 December 2009
166377LV00008B/24/P